THE
ELEPHANTS
of STYLE

A Trunkload of Tips
on the Big Issues and Gray
Areas of Contemporary
American English

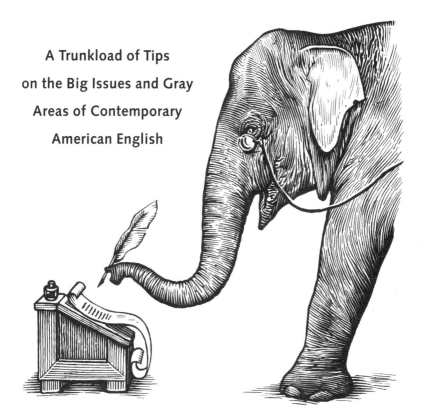

Bill Walsh

McGraw·Hill

New York   Chicago   San Francisco   Lisbon   London   Madrid   Mexico City
Milan   New Delhi   San Juan   Seoul   Singapore   Sydney   Toronto

The McGraw·Hill Companies

Library of Congress Cataloging-in-Publication Data

Walsh, Bill (William F.)
      The elephants of style : a trunkload of tips on the big issues and gray areas of
contemporary American English / by Bill Walsh.
            p.   cm.
      ISBN 0-07-142268-4 (alk. paper)
      1. English language—United States—Usage—Handbooks, manuals, etc.
      2. English language—United States—Style—Handbooks, manuals, etc.
      3. English language—United States—Usage—Humor.   4. English language—
United States—Style—Humor.   I. Title.

PE2827.W35   2004
428'.00973—dc22   2003017004

Parts of Elephant No. 10 originally appeared in the newsletter Copy Editor.

2 3 4 5 6 7 8 9 0   FGR/FGR   3 2 1 0 9 8 7 6 5 4

ISBN 0-07-142268-4

McGraw-Hill books are available at special quantity discounts to use as premiums and
sales promotions, or for use in corporate training programs. For more information, please
write to the Director of Special Sales, Professional Publishing, McGraw-Hill, Two Penn
Plaza, New York, NY 10121-2298. Or contact your local bookstore.

This book is printed on acid-free paper.

For my mom, Molly Chilinski, who didn't raise no dummies

CONTENTS

Acknowledgments

It wouldn't be incorrect to call this book a one-man effort. But then there are all the women who deserve credit: my agent, Sheree Bykofsky, and her associates, Janet Rosen and Megan Buckley; my editor at McGraw-Hill, Judith McCarthy; my Washington Post colleagues Nancy McKeon and Autumn Brewington for their proofreading assistance; and most of all my wife, Jacqueline Dupree, who endured countless nights of staying upstairs and being as quiet as possible while I sweated over my computer in the downstairs den.

Considering my harsh words about plagiarism, I must come clean and admit that I wasn't born with an opinion on split infinitives or the hyphenation of compound modifiers. I take pride in making original observations about the language (or "concocting new maxims," to paraphrase one amateur critic), but my views have been influenced by countless teachers, colleagues and fellow authors. Barbara Wallraff, my competitor on the bookstore shelves and my editor when I write for the Copy Editor newsletter, has been especially generous when I've needed second opinions. John McIntyre and Merrill Perlman also continue to shape my thinking.

Some of the quotations that begin the chapters came from my memory, my music collection or my personal library; others, I found and cross-checked using a variety of online sources.

My bibliography lists the books that I have found most useful; any omissions should be considered not a snub but rather an illustration of the limits of my budget and my shelf space.

INTRODUCTION

What We Talk About
When We Talk About Style

Who needs action when you've got words?
—The Meat Puppets

"What's our style on . . . ?"

Spend time in a newsroom, a magazine office or anywhere else that publishing takes place and you'll hear that question. Strictly speaking, style refers to a choice of one correct alternative over another for the sake of consistency (*canceled* over *cancelled*, *nine* over *9*, *OK* over *O.K.* or *okay*) and an appropriate level of formality (what gets abbreviated, what gets capitalized and which typographical niceties are used). Often, however, the word *style* is used loosely to refer to correctness in spelling, grammar, syntax, usage or even matters of fact. Stylebooks cheerfully take on this broader definition of style, and "The Elements of Style," the Strunk-and-White classic whose title I've misappropriated, tackles even the broadest definition of writing style—style as in flair! Elan! Panache!

I, too, will touch on style in all its forms, with an eye toward the current state of the art. There's no denying that language evolves, that what is incorrect today could be correct tomorrow. Some in the "descriptivist" school of language analysis take this point to extremes, arguing that there is no wrong; there is what is. "Prescriptivists" tend to resist this evolution, insisting that some widespread usages are wrong because they've always been wrong before.

I'm a prescriptivist, as you may have guessed when you picked up a usage manual with my name on it, but I consider myself a sensible prescriptivist. Call me other names if you like, but if you, too, are in the business of writing, even if you think it's arrogant to condemn a perfectly understandable bit of prose as "wrong," you have to answer one big question: *Do you want to look stupid?*

Language evolves, but at each instant in that evolution there will be ways of writing that will strike educated readers as ignorant. All but the most namby-pamby of descriptivists will agree that some things in writing (*I is an writer*) are understandable but pretty much incorrect (or is it *differently correct?*). The Elephants in "The Elephants of Style" are the biggies, the major usage points that educated people sometimes disagree about (or should that be *about which educated people sometimes disagree?*). Any usage guide is at best a snapshot of contemporary usage at the time when the book was truly contemporary.

Among the opinionated, the speed of language evolution is a lot like speed on the highway. George Carlin's observation comes to mind: "Why is it that anybody who drives slower than you is a moron, but anybody who drives faster than you is a maniac?" This applies to style as in usage and to style as in flair. Am I being too much of a purist in enforcing an increasingly little-observed point of grammar? Am I being too much of a spoilsport in pooh-poohing an attempt at fun in favor of just-the-facts-ma'am?

I wince at *teenager* with a hyphen, but I wince at *e-mail* without a hyphen. I wince at writing that's bright-and-breezy-magaziney, but I also wince a little at the mantra "simple, declarative sentences."

I even wince at *ten, eleven* and *twelve*, but I know I shouldn't—the newspaper style dictum that numbers of two or more digits should be written as numerals is completely arbitrary.

I wince at sentences that begin with *However*, because Strunk and White caution against such a usage, although that's one of the few arguments in "The Elements of Style" that strike me as unconvincing. (Lessons learned early are hard to unlearn, even when they're wrong.)

Who died and put me in charge of the English language? Fair question. As anyone who's been involved in putting together a house stylebook knows, there's something to be said for a benevolent dictator rather than rule by committee. In English, however, we have a particularly anarchic form of rule by committee: descriptive guidance from dictionaries and simple observation, plus prescriptive guidance from mavens of varying degrees of authority, living and dead. If our language, like French, were under bureaucratic control, we could clear up a lot of widely debated questions. If I were in charge, I would dispense with this *he or she, him or her, his or her* nonsense and bless *they, them, their, theirs* as acceptable singular pronouns. I would tell the purists that *host* can be a verb, *gender* isn't just a language term anymore and *hopefully* can indeed mean "it is hoped that."

Such a bureaucracy would be run by someone else, though, so I suppose I'm thankful for the status quo: a confederacy of wincers who can't agree on what to wince about. The best we can hope for, and my goal in this book, is to find a consensus on what doesn't look stupid—at least for now.

If my first book, "Lapsing Into a Comma," is a reference for editors and writers, "The Elephants of Style" is a reference for writers and editors. In "Lapsing" I stressed obscure points of usage—matters not covered by other manuals and contrarian takes on widely covered matters. In "Elephants," I take a step back and look at the big issues, the frequently asked questions of American English, before lapsing back into some little issues in a second installment of the Curmudgeon's Stylebook. The first book covered at least some of the big issues, of course, so there is some overlap.

As the book goes along, the Elephants get less basic, so if you've mastered the easy stuff you may want to skip ahead. But don't be so quick to say you've mastered the easy stuff.

STYLE NOTES

What style to follow for a book about style? I made my choices with clarity and consistency in mind.

It goes without saying that I want the book to be internally consistent, but I also wanted to stay consistent with "Lapsing Into a Comma" and with my Web site, The Slot (www.theslot.com). In "Lapsing" I took a populist stance against some of the conventions of formal publishing. So, while I am writing for writers and editors of all types, I am staying close to my newspaper roots by:

- Using quotation marks rather than italics for such things as book and movie titles.
- Skipping the "serial comma" in most cases.
- Using hyphens where most stylebooks use en dashes.
- Using no accent marks or other diacriticals.

But I depart from Associated Press style, which is used by most newspapers, on many issues. In addition to the use of italics discussed above (AP style uses no italics, because the newswires and some newspapers lack the technology to produce them), the two most notable departures are:

- My dashes—em dashes—are "tight," meaning they abut the words they separate rather than being flanked by spaces.
- I use an apostrophe and an *s*, not just an apostrophe, to form the possessive of singular nouns ending in *s*: *the genus's characteristics, Harlan Sanders's chicken.*

REMEMBER THAT YOU'RE NOT USING A TYPEWRITER

Style Begins With Form and Format

I just sit at a typewriter and curse a bit.

—P.G. WODEHOUSE ON HIS WRITING TECHNIQUE

If you *are* using a typewriter, skip to Elephant No. 2.

I'm not a big fan of the idea of books and classes about "writing for the Web" and similar nonsense. Writing is writing, on a Gateway or with a glitter pen. *Formatting*, on the other hand, does change.

The big formatting difference between writing with a typewriter and writing with a computer may surprise you. Are you still putting two spaces after periods, exclamation points, question marks and colons? You shouldn't be. Some places are still clinging to this typewriter convention, no doubt, but as a standard operating procedure it went out with the IBM Selectric. In fact, many publishing systems treat two or three

Also, Remember That
You're in the United States

Unless you're not. (Tell you what: If you're in England or somewhere else that uses British English *and* you're using a typewriter, keep reading for your amusement, but don't bother taking notes.)

I'll discuss some differences in spelling and usage later, but one technical issue looms large (and this is a very frequently asked question):

In American English, commas and periods adjacent to quotation marks go *inside* the quotation marks. Semicolons and colons go outside. Is this logical? Not really; it's just the way it's done.

If you're looking for logic, look to the question mark, the exclamation point or British English. Question marks and exclamation points go inside or outside quotation marks depending on whether the questioner/exclaimer is the person being quoted or the writer. British English applies the same rationale to commas and periods. (There is never a logical reason to put a colon or semicolon inside an adjacent quotation mark.)

CORRECT ON BOTH SIDES OF THE ATLANTIC: *He said "yes"!* (The writer is being emphatic.)

CORRECT ON BOTH SIDES OF THE ATLANTIC: *He said "no!"*
(The person being quoted was emphatic.)

CORRECT IN BRITISH ENGLISH ONLY: *We saw "Gone With the Wind"*. (The period isn't part of the title.)

CORRECT IN AMERICAN ENGLISH ONLY: *We saw "Gone With the Wind."* (The period goes inside. It just does.)

---

or 10,000 spaces as a single space. So does hypertext markup language, or HTML, the coding standard for the Web.

All right, so you were in the groove of hitting the space bar twice. Good luck breaking that habit. Now let's talk about word formatting. Are you still underlining book titles? It's easy enough to produce underlined type on a computer (on most word processors, ctrl b is bold, ctrl i is italic and ctrl u is underline), but why would you want to? Underlining is to typed and handwritten papers what italics are to more formal publishing. If you're older than 30 or so, your high-school papers probably talk about <u>The Grapes of Wrath</u> and <u>Lord of the Flies</u>, but today we have computers and italics, and we might as well use them. Today, the only widespread use of underlined text is to denote clickable links in Web documents. (The newspaper convention, which I use as a newspaperman and which was also a response to a technical inability to use italics, is quotation marks for book, movie and other titles.)

On a typewriter, you use two hyphens to indicate a dash (that's *em* dash, for those of you who also use the highfalutin en dash). In the computer world, unfortunately, making a proper dash can be complicated. You can go ahead and keep using the two-hyphen approach, which will be technically correct but lacking in polish. Some word-processing software is kind enough to automatically turn two adjoining hyphens into a dash or at least to allow that feature to be programmed. Otherwise, you have to figure out what combination of keystrokes and mouse clicks your word processor requires.

Another typographical nicety that adds both polish and the occasional headache to computer-produced documents is the idea of "smart" apostrophes and quotation marks, also known as "curly quotes." On a typewriter and in the standard computer character set, apostrophes and quotation marks are essentially hash marks, vertical and symmetrical. An open-quote is the same as a close-quote. With a fancy word-processing program, however, apostrophes look like commas. Open-quote marks look like upside-down-and-backward commas. Computer keyboards must produce these typographical marvels without extra keys, so the software must be "smart" enough to guess which punctuation mark you're after. Usually it does a good job, but sometimes you have to trick it. Maybe you're writing a movie review for a newspaper (they use quotation marks in this case, remember) and you want to mention Woody Allen's post-"Hannah and Her Sisters" slump. Your computer thinks open-quote marks occur only after spaces, which is generally correct, so it might give you *post-"Hannah*. To get *post-"Hannah* without wrestling with an "insert special character" menu, you might need to start with a space between *post-* and *"Hannah* and then go back and close it up.

Finally, it's worth mentioning that the computer is not a toy. It can do a lot of cute little things, but that doesn't mean it's a good idea to take advantage of such things. If you're writing for your own amusement or printing a document yourself, go ahead and use the subscript on H_2O and the superscript on $e = mc^2$. But if you'll be turning your document over to someone else for publication, there's a good chance that different hoops need to be jumped through to render such effects. So be sure to ask. What looks like a cute little 2 on your computer may look like something different or even alien on your editor's. And resist the temptation to use obscure symbols. If you're writing for American readers, for instance, the style on the British pound and the euro is *pounds* and *euros*, not the symbols that represent those currencies.

Also, forget about the © and the ® and the TM. Those decorations are for lawyers, not writers, unless you're writing advertising copy that mentions a competitor's product.

One more thing, just for the old-timers: Some typewriters didn't have a 1 (one), so we used the *l* (lowercase *L*). All computers have the 1 (one), and in some typefaces the *l* (lowercase *L*) looks nothing like a number, so please use the 1 (one).

LETTERS OF THE LAW

Common Missteps in Spelling

A burro *is an ass. A* burrow *is a hole in the ground. As a journalist you are expected to know the difference.*

—The United Press International Stylebook

In second grade I delighted in using alternate spellings, even on spelling tests, and *grey* served me well. If you're a grown-up and style is of any concern to you, however, you need to forget such phrases as "alternate spelling" and "either spelling is acceptable." Establishing a style means picking a spelling and sticking to it. There are no shades of "grey."

Being a writer or an editor also means being conversant with the hard-to-spell words that everybody knows are hard to spell. Literate people master the M-I-S-S-I-S-S-I-P-P-I thing in childhood, and they should have *minuscule* and *consensus* and *supersede* at their fingertips as adults, even if not-

so-tricky words still require a trip to the dictionary. Here's
your memorization assignment:

accommodate
acknowledgment
ad nauseam
aficionado
Albuquerque
Ali, Muhammad
allotted
anoint
barbiturate
battalion
Cage, Nicolas
camaraderie
Cincinnati
Connors, Jimmy
consensus
demonstrator
ecstasy
embarrassment
emperor
existence
Gandhi, Mohandas, Indira, Rajiv
grammar
Giuliani, Rudolph
harassment
idiosyncrasy
impostor
inadvertent
indispensable

inoculate
irresistible
irritable
judgment
liaison
liquefy
millennium
minuscule
mischievous
newsstand
nickel
occurrence
ophthalmology
parishioner
pastime
perseverance
Philippines
poinsettia
Portuguese
Procter & Gamble Co.
protester
restaurateur
Riviera
roommate
sacrilegious
separate
stratagem
Streisand, Barbra
supersede
threshold

PICK ONE

There are misspellings, and then there are errors of style regarding spelling. Choosing *advisor* when your publication calls for *adviser* cannot be considered as serious an error as *miniscule* or *concensus* or *supercede*, but for style purposes it is an error. The following is a list of American English spellings that are preferred by a *consensus* of reputable publications:

aesthetic, not *esthetic*
archaeology, not *archeology*
ax, not *axe*
bandanna, not *bandana*
barbecue, not *barbeque* or *bar-B-Q*
dialogue, not *dialog*
dietitian, not *dietician*
employee, not *employe*
fjord, not *fiord*
flier, not *flyer*
gray, not *grey*
ketchup, not *catsup*
kidnapped, not *kidnaped*
marijuana, not *marihuana*
Muslim, not *Moslem*
mustache, not *moustache*
percent, not *per cent*
saguaro, not *sahuaro*
sheik, not *sheikh*
theater, not *theatre*
Vietnam, not *Viet Nam*

You'll want to check with the publication you're writing or editing for before committing to the preferred spellings. And then there are the very close calls, on which a particular publication's preference would be hard to guess. Definitely ask the question on *catalog/catalogue, ambience/ambiance, adviser/ advisor, crawfish/crayfish, OK/O.K./okay, racket/racquet* and *doughnut/donut*. (I've listed the AP preference first in each case.)

IN GENERAL . . .

If you're looking for all-purpose guidelines on spelling beyond "look it up," keep in mind that we're dealing with *English* here. English spelling is all about oddities and exceptions, so I'll present just one general guideline:

When you're adding *-ed* or *-ing* or *-er* to a verb, double a single final consonant only if the stress is on the final syllable. So, at least in American English, *can*cel becomes *canceled*, and *trav*el becomes *traveler*, but pa*trol* becomes *patrolling*. Having said that, I will present my theory that errors in that department stem not so much from ignorance of that guideline as from a llove of the lletter *L*. Somebody who doesn't know the syllable test might write about *marshalling* one's forces, but how do you explain the white-hatted Old West guy with the star-shaped badge being called a *marshall*? Llong llive llamas!

Did I mention the part about English and exceptions? Well, the syllable test won't help you on *kid*napped or *wor*shipped or *trans*ferred. (The Ameri*can* Heri*tage* Diction*ary* says trans*ferred* is more common, but who in the world ever pronounced it that way? The late George Plimpton? The fake-British Madonna? The fake-German Kathleen Turner?)

Worshiped doesn't bother me, but *kidnaped* is flawed in that it suggests a rhyme with *nape*. You'll find both alternate spellings, by the way, in the archives of the largely abandoned simplified-spelling experiment carried on by Chicago Tribune Publisher Robert McCormick from the 1930s to the 1970s. In another such relic, I've found that writers and editors of a certain age tend to write *employe*, or at least let it slip by. *Cigaret* is another one I remember reading as a child in the '60s. A few publications, no doubt, continue to cling to those letter-saving conventions.

WHAT'S UP?

All About Capitalization

She felt in italics and thought in capitals.

—Henry James

Capitalization sounds easy—essentially, everything should be lowercase except sentence beginnings and proper nouns—but within those guidelines is room for endless variation and confusion.

Titles

Take this sentence: *I saw the President go by.* That capital *P* is either a common error or a sign that the writer is writing for a formal publication. In most newspapers and magazines, such titles are capitalized only when they're used directly before a name. President Bush is *the president*; Pope John Paul II is *the pope*. And when I say directly before the name, I mean directly. Please don't use what I call the high-school-yearbook comma.

 CORRECT: *Student Council President Muffy Tepperman will speak.* (*President* is used as a title.)

ALSO CORRECT: *The Student Council president, Muffy Tepperman, will speak.* (*President* is used as a description, and the president's name is in apposition—that is, set off with commas.)

PROBABLY A STYLE ERROR: *The Student Council President, Muffy Tepperman, will speak.* (Most stylebooks call for a lowercase *p*.)

STUPID HIGH-SCHOOL-YEARBOOK COMMA: *Student Council President, Muffy Tepperman, will speak.* (Omitting the *The* sets us up for the correct use of a capitalized title. But then the sentence goes and does the apposition thing. For apposition to work correctly, the sentence must make sense without the material between the commas. *Student Council President will speak* does not make sense, unless it's a headline.)

EVEN STUPIDER, AND PROBABLY EVEN MORE COMMON: *Student Council President, Muffy Tepperman will speak.* (Apposition is incorrect here, because there's no *The*, but if you're going to attempt apposition, at least use both commas.)

For some reason, the presence of the word *attorney* seems to make writers forget everything they know about capitalization. But the usual rules apply: In all but the most formal publications, District Attorney Adam Schiff is *the district attorney*. Assistant U.S. Attorney Ana Rivera is *the assistant U.S. attorney*. Attorney General Dan Larson is *the attorney general*. With *office*, capitalize either all the words or none of them (apart from *U.S.*, of course). *U.S. Attorney's Office* and *U.S. attorney's office* are both valid style decisions, but *U.S. Attorney's office* is an error.

TITLES VS. JOB DESCRIPTIONS

The rule for capitalizing a person's job title does not apply to general job descriptions: *Vice President Dick Cheney, janitor Gus Henkel*. In-between cases can be tricky—*manager* might be a formal title at the corporate level but a job description at a movie theater or a gas station.

Publications vary when it comes to the sanctity of titles as titles. A word or two before a title can demote that title to a job description. In most newspapers you'll see titles rendered like this: *French President Jacques Chirac, Chicago Mayor Richard M. Daley*.

To capitalize *president* and *mayor* in such a usage is not technically correct, but it's a compromise that all but the most formal publications have settled on to avoid dragging readers, writers and editors through a style morass. Ultimately I agree, but such dragging is my job. Here goes:

Chirac's title is *president*, not *French president*, so once you've slapped a modifier (*French*) on the title, it becomes a mere description and no longer merits capitalization. To look at it another way, *French* modifies *president*, period. If *president* is being used as a title, *President Jacques Chirac* holds together as a unit. Then what is *French* doing? *President* is already spoken for, so all *French* can hope to do is modify that entire unit. But that's not the intention in *French President Jacques Chirac*; the meaning isn't simply to point out that President Jacques Chirac is French. The meaning is that he's the president of France, or *the French president*. So *president* belongs to *French*, not to *Jacques Chirac*, and isn't truly being used as a title. Therefore: *French president Jacques Chirac*.

The New York Times stylebook follows this reasoning, cautioning writers to "not make the place name part of the title." Its example: *Mayor Stacy K. Bildots of Chicago*, not *Chicago Mayor Stacy K. Bildots*.

The Chicago Manual of Style gives the same advice, calling for *President Francois Mitterrand of France*, and even goes so far as to specify the lowercase in *French president Francois Mitterrand*.

My admittedly picky problem with the New York Times-Chicago approach is that it divorces the title from its context. *Stacy K. Bildots, mayor of Chicago*, is clear, but *Mayor Stacy K. Bildots of Chicago* tells me only that Bildots is a mayor and is from Chicago. What is Bildots the mayor of? You could infer that it means mayor of Chicago, but it doesn't actually say that. Same with *Chicago's Mayor Stacy K. Bildots*. (Such references seem clearer to me in the plural, where the *of* clause could be read as applying to *mayors*: *Mayors Anthony Williams of Washington and Martin O'Malley of Baltimore*.)

The Associated Press Stylebook doesn't specifically call for such a capital letter in the *French President Jacques Chirac* case, but that policy can be inferred from its endorsement of *former President Ford*. The Washington Post, which doesn't get nearly as picky as the New York Times on the issue, specifically calls for lowercasing a title after *former*, because *former president* is obviously a description; *former president* applies to *Ford*, as opposed to *former* applying to *President Ford*. For the same reason, the Post calls for full names for former presidents. He was *President Ford*, but now he's *former president Gerald R. Ford*.

AP calls for lowercase on all references for *professor* and *coach*, probably to avoid the morass. Sports coaches are so deified in the United States, however, that many publications override this policy, and you get the obviously faulty *football Coach Steve Spurrier*. A sensible compromise on *coach* would capitalize it when unadorned but lowercase it when it's attached to a modifier: *Coach Steve Spurrier, football coach Steve Spurrier*.

The Washington Post stylebook offers that sort of ruling on *professor*, which it not only capitalizes but also abbreviates as a title: *Prof. Pierre LeGrand of Georgetown University; Georgetown University French professor Pierre LeGrand; former American University chemistry professor George Brown*.

But what about *Redskins Coach Steve Spurrier* or *Georgetown University Prof. Pierre LeGrand* or even *U.S. Marine Corps Sgt. Vince Carter*? Those examples get to the heart of the *French President Jacques Chirac* problem, and to me they illustrate a reasonable place to draw the line. *French* doesn't alter the character of *president* the way *former* does, and *Redskins* leaves the title *coach* intact, unlike *football*. So it would be *Coach Steve Spurrier, Washington Coach Steve Spurrier* and *Redskins Coach Steve Spurrier* but *new coach Steve Spurrier, outspoken coach Steve Spurrier* and *NFL coach Steve Spurrier*. Once adjectives pile on, default to lowercase: *new Redskins coach Steve Spurrier*. Similarly:

President Jacques Chirac, French President Jacques Chirac, longtime president Jacques Chirac, irascible president Jacques Chirac.

Sgt. Vince Carter, Marine Sgt. Vince Carter, drill sergeant Vince Carter, hot-tempered sergeant Vince Carter.

And, please, don't try *law school Dean Steve Rabinowitz.* As a general rule, if what modifies a title isn't capitalized, the title isn't eligible for capitalization either.

Note that even the New York Times isn't completely true to its policy of capitalizing only the official title: It makes exceptions for *State Senator Morgan R. Daan* and *City Comptroller Pat C. Berenich.*

And then there's the *police* thing. AP style would be *police Sgt. Joe Friday,* and most newspapers infer that *officer* would work the same way: *police Officer Bill Gannon,* which grates on the eyes because *police officer* is such a familiar expression. I don't like *police sergeant Joe Friday* any more than *police Sgt. Joe Friday,* but I do think *police officer* should be considered a job description whenever those words occur in sequence, and I don't think *police* should be capitalized willy-nilly. So write around it when you can, and go for *Los Angeles Police Department Sgt. Joe Friday* and *Officer Bill Gannon* if you want to invoke the *French President Jacques Chirac* exception.

FALSE TITLES

Speaking of titles, you may have heard the term *false title.* What that means is a label in front of a person's name that acts like a title but is actually a description. Title: *General Manager Brian Cashman.* False title: *pitcher Roger Clemens.* This is not usually a capitalization issue, although Time magazine used to capitalize false titles. One issue that remains, however, is whether false titles need to be "fixed." The New York Times, as far as I know, is unique among newspapers in that it follows the formal style of turning false titles into true descriptions by using *the*. The Times makes a limited exception for sports positions, so *pitcher Roger Clemens* would be OK, but *actor Sean Connery* would be *the actor Sean Connery*.

This may seem stilted, even wacky, because false titles are so widely used elsewhere, but you'll see the logic if you look at the use of similar labels for things other than people. Most good writers and editors would prefer *the trade association Plastics Forever* and *the men's magazine SuaveGent* to *trade association Plastics Forever* and *men's magazine SuaveGent*. So let the level of formality you're going for dictate your position on false titles, but even if you decide that false titles are just fine, be aware of the reasoning behind that strange *the*.

LOGOS

The seemingly simple issue of capitalizing proper nouns has gotten muddied somewhat by *e.e. cummings* and *k.d. lang* and "*thirtysomething*" and cutesy all-lowercase company names. The short answer is that the usual rules apply. You're a writer, not a logo replicator, and the capitalization of proper nouns is one of the most basic principles of English orthography. (See the "What's in a nAME?" sidebar in this Elephant for a point-by-point rebuttal of the objections you'll run into when you try to enforce this principle.)

In what I call the de Gaulle exception, you might want to let slide proper nouns that don't begin with capitals but introduce them within a letter or two: *eBay, iMac.* But, for the love of Strunk, don't interpret this to mean that a sentence can ever, ever begin with a lowercase letter. The sentences-begin-with-capitals rule trumps all: *IMacs are for sale on eBay.*

And don't bother getting worked up over MidWord caps, as long as the capital letter corresponds with a new word or syllable: *NationsBank* and *CompuServe* are fine; *ARTnews* is not, unless it's pronounced "A-R-T news."

And . . .

Some other capitalization issues:

SEASONS

It's *winter, spring, summer* and *fall,* not *Winter, Spring, Summer* and *Fall.*

ACADEMIC SUBJECTS

You major in biology, not Biology. (English or French, of course, would be a different story.)

TERMS WITH COMMONLY KNOWN ACRONYMS OR ABBREVIATIONS

The IRA (uppercase) is *the Irish Republican Army* (uppercase), but *an IRA* (uppercase) is *an individual retirement account*

Everything's Generic

For those who thought they'd seen everything when it comes to the mindless genericization of trade names (*kleenex, xerox* and the other usual suspects, plus some newbies, such as *hotmail* for any free e-mail service and *power point* as though it's a term and not a trademark), I think I have a new low. The following sentence, about a remodeled hotel, is from a community newspaper, not a big-time publication, so I apologize in advance for being so mean. And now I'll be mean.

> *General Manager, Laura Schofield, calls it a "pottery barn/ retail look," which when translated means the new decor has nothing to do with "no surprises" and everything to do with such indulgences as data ports at the desks, sybaritic baths, and kitchenettes equipped with refrigerators and microwave ovens.*

A *pottery barn* look? *Hold everything!* Did the editors fall into *the gap*? They should be tied up with *linens and things* and sent to *bed, bath and beyond*!

Do the people who wrote and edited that sentence think *pottery barn* refers to a barn in which pottery is stored? Uppercasing *Pottery Barn* would repair the passage if the comparison actually made sense, but what does the Pottery

Barn home-furnishings chain have to do with data ports and kitchenettes?

Similarly, some wire-service reports about an antitrust ruling against 3M Corp. said the dispute involved a competitor's assertion that 3M had a monopoly on "scotch tape." The company does indeed have a monopoly on *Scotch* tape, the same way Coca-Cola Co. has a monopoly on Coke. Scotch is a brand name for 3M's popular transparent tape; it's not called Scotch tape because it was invented in Scotland or smells like Glenfiddich. LePage's and other competitors make *transparent tape*.

Not quite as stupid (because the words sort of make sense if you don't know any better) but more shocking (because this is from the New York Times):

> *"VeggieTales" is not the only best seller to receive a mighty push from discount chains like Wal-Mart, Target and Kmart, and price clubs like Costco and Wal-Mart's Sam's Club.*

Price club, of course, is not a term meaning "membership store with low prices." Price Club, with capital letters, was the name of such a chain until it was folded into Costco. The name sprang from an aptonym: Although low prices were certainly part of the equation, the founder's name was Sol Price. The generic term for such stores would be *warehouse clubs* or something like that.

To write *Sam's Club price clubs* and *Costco price clubs*, as the Times writer did later in the same article, is especially ridiculous. To recycle an analogy I used when I saw the phrase *ziploc baggies*, it's like writing *Have a Pepsi coke!*

(lowercase). If you're *SOL*, you're *shit outta luck.* The existence of an acronym or initialism doesn't necessarily mean those initials are capped when the term is spelled out.

COMPASS DIRECTIONS

Lowercase *north, south, east* and *west* unless they represent regions: *I moved west because I was tired of the East.* When a direction is a modifier in a place name, capitalize it if it's well known to your readership. *Southern California* is always up, but *northern Virginia* is down unless you're writing for people in or near that region. Caution: If that *-ern* is missing, it's a good sign you're dealing with a region name that should be capitalized. *South Florida* has probably attained *Southern California* status, but if you're going to write *East Tennessee*, capitalize it. Use *eastern Tennessee* if you don't like the capital *E*.

When the North, the South, the East and the West become adjectives, most publications retain the capitalization. Buford T. Pusser is *a Southern sheriff* in most publications, though the Washington Post would lowercase *southern.*

VANITY CAPITALIZATION

If you're writing for a company or a university, the style may be to write *Company* and *University* on all references. At a newspaper, perhaps you capitalize *The* in your own publication's name but nobody else's.

THE *The*

Remember that a capitalized *The* is part of the name it's attached to; it cannot serve any other function in the sentence. So even if you capitalize the *The* in *The Post*, you must write *I accepted the Post job*, not *I accepted The Post job*. (*Job* needs its own *the*.) Partly to avoid such complications, many publications choose to lowercase all uses of *the* at the beginning of a name. I don't think it's possible, however, to follow that policy religiously. If there's a magazine called The Truth, that *The* is integral to the name in a way that the *The* in *The New York Times* is not.

ACRONYMS

First, a definition. An acronym is a *word* made up of initials or syllables from a combination of other words. *HUD* is an acronym, because it's pronounced as a word: "hud." *HHS* is an initialism, not an acronym, because it's pronounced letter by letter: "H-H-S."

Now back to capitalization. A few common-noun acronyms have truly become words and lost their capitalization altogether—*scuba* comes from *self-contained underwater breathing apparatus*; *snafu* comes from . . . well, let's just say *snafu* is best avoided. As for capitalized acronyms, ideally they should be all caps only if each letter actually stands for a word. *NATO* is the North Atlantic Treaty Organization, but what the U.S. Army calls *CENTCOM* should be *Centcom* in a well-edited publication. It stands for Central Command, not, say, Collection of Enlisted Ninjas Taking Care to Obliterate the Masses.

Unless you're deeply enough committed to this principle that you don't mind eliciting some head-scratching, however, you do need to allow for a grandfather clause of sorts for a few well-known acronyms that shouldn't be all caps but have been written that way so extensively as to be entrenched. *START* and *START II*, for instance, stand for Strategic Arms Reduction Treaty or Strategic Arms Reduction Talks; because the first *T* doesn't stand for a word, strictly speaking these acronyms should be written as *Start* and *Start II*. But the grandfather clause, and the parallel with *SALT* (the Strategic Arms Limitation Talks/Treaty), presents a strong argument for letting the errant capitalization go.

Some stylebooks establish an arbitrary length at which an acronym can no longer be all caps. For the New York Times and the Wall Street Journal it's five letters or more, so *Unicef*, *Unesco* and other acronyms that most people are used to seeing in all caps are treated differently in those newspapers.

Of course, I'm writing from an American English viewpoint. British English, for the most part, treats true acronyms as words and not initials. In British, NATO is *Nato*.

CAPITALS AND HYPHENS

A proper noun constitutes a single modifier no matter how many words it contains, so the idea of compound-modifier hyphenation does not apply. A source who is off the record is *an off-the-record source*, but a source at the White House is *a White House source*, not *a White-House source*. Outside the proper noun, the usual rules apply: *a White House-led investigation*.

What's in a nAME?

As I discussed at length in "Lapsing Into a Comma," decisions about capitalization are ultimately the responsibility of writers and editors, not corporate hucksters. With companies and Web sites and bands adorning their names with unconventional capitalization and decorative punctuation, the following is a point-by-point rebuttal to the inevitable protest that goes something like "But *funky*WEB!dudes!! is their *trademark!*"

Everything you need to know about capitalization you learned in kindergarten. That might be an exaggeration, but the point is that the most basic of capitalization rules are not to be trifled with. Proper nouns are capitalized. The all-caps style is for initial-based abbreviations. Use all caps for names that aren't initialisms and your writing will look like a cheesy news release:

The sponsors include NIKE and VISA.

At the other extreme, the all-lowercase fad deprives readers of the most basic of visual cues:

A $12 million merger announced Monday will unite allman-nerofthings.com and youdbetterbelieveit.com, two of Pitts-burgh's fastest-growing Internet companies.

Readers glancing at this paragraph—and you'd better believe that readers glance—will decide whether it's worth reading based on three words: *Monday*, *Pittsburgh* and *Internet*. The proper-nouns-are-capped rule is there for a reason: It makes the important things stand out.

Funky logos are nothing new. In the old days, battles on this front usually involved companies that insisted on being identified in all caps. The uppercase treatment, after all, makes something STAND OUT. But there weren't as many battles as there are today, because copy editors and even writers knew that logos are logos and English is English. "You want all caps?" an ink-stained wretch with a green eyeshade might have asked. "Go buy an ad!"

But then something changed, and I'm not exactly sure when or why. Maybe it was the decline of the green eyeshade. Maybe up-and-coming copy editors of the 1970s and '80s figured that if Adidas and "Thirtysomething" (not a company name, but the point's the same) wanted their names lower-cased—obscured rather than trumpeted—that didn't quite merit the "Go buy an ad" response. But this capitulation has been oddly selective. Plenty of TV shows and movies before "Thirtysomething" had lowercased logos, and I've never seen *Macy's* lowercased in print—but there it is, not only lower-cased but also with a star where the apostrophe should be, on the side of every store. Do we need to send reporters and copy editors on field trips?

By the way, for those who need a refresher, the AP style rule on company names is that all caps is used only if each letter is pronounced as a separate letter. So CSX is *CSX*, but the snappy little ARCOs and PEPCOs are initial-capped, even if they are each-letter-stands-for-something acronyms. Usually they don't even meet this standard: Arco is (or at least was) Atlantic Richfield Co.; Pepco was Potomac Electric Power Co.—so what do those O's stand for?

Logos don't even necessarily represent what a company wants to be called. Look at Macy's, or should I say macy*s? (You'll be doing a lot of looking at Macy's during my little essay, unless by some miracle on 34th Street I send you to Gimbels. The Macy's case illustrates almost every one of my points.) Heck, look all around you. You might be hard-pressed to find a consumer product or showbiz title whose packaging or publicity doesn't take liberties with the rules of capitalization. But does that mean we have to write *"THREE'S COMPANY"* or *KRAFT Macaroni and Cheese DINNER*? Of course not. Better yet, look at this excerpt from a letter that an actual flack sent to copy chiefs across the D.C. area:

> *Just a reminder that we are Inova Health System, not INOVA. Inova isn't an acronym. Inova is just a name, with roots in the words "Northern Virginia," where we were born and raised, and "innovative," which is what we try to be. Much of the confusion comes from our logo (see above). In the logo, all the letters are capitalized for stylistic reasons. But I've yet to see an article where INOVA HEALTH SYSTEM appears. That looks ridiculous to everyone.*

Inova is one of the good guys. I'd like to introduce you to one of the bad guys, though with all due respect I should mention that this guy is deceased:

US West, which was its own company until it was bought by Qwest Communications, simultaneously promulgated a ridiculously rendered logo (USWEST) and a ridiculously rendered name (U S West, which I suppose we should have pronounced "U [dramatic pause] S West"). Which brings me to my next point:

A lot of companies can't decide what they call themselves. I've seen Web sites where a company's name was rendered at least three different ways. I've seen many, many Web sites with two different renderings of a company name—US West is one; another pretty much defunct company, Erols, was another. Erols still exists as a brand name, so you can point your browser at www.erols.com and see for yourself: The title bar says "Erol's." Elsewhere it says "Erols," without the apostrophe. Then there are J.C. Penney and the new Exxon Mobil. These are the way the company names exist in corporate officialdom, but company flacks would have us bow to the logos and write:

> *J.C. Penney Co. Inc. said sales increased last year at its JCPenney stores.*

> *Exxon Mobil Corp. plans to open 500 new ExxonMobil service stations.*

Come on, guys, pick one. If you hate those periods and those spaces so much, tell it to the Securities and Exchange Commission. Until then, publications run by grown-ups will tell you where to stick your logos.

Don't worry about crashing the Internet. World Wide Web addresses can be case-sensitive, but domain names, the part of the address that ends in *.com* or *.org* or whatever, are not. So you won't be sending readers on a detour if you capitalize the first letter of a dot-com company's name.

Stylistically, however, it is important to decide whether you're dealing with a name or an address. Internet addresses that are simply addresses should be lowercased, but if the name and the address are functionally the same (typing the name Amazon.com into a browser, for example, will get a Web user to the address www.amazon.com), use the name. But don't use a Web address to invent a Web-site name that doesn't exist:

WRONG: *Bill Walsh runs a Web site called TheSlot.com.*

RIGHT: *Bill Walsh runs a Web site called The Slot (www.theslot.com).*

Punctuation is not decoration. This is a multifaceted issue, and although I remain a purist, I will admit that it presents some difficult decisions on where we, as editors, should draw the line. In referring to the Macy's logo I write *macy*s* with an asterisk. It's actually a five-sided star, the good ol' American kind, but that's not a standard print character, and many if not most newspapers would run into a problem reproducing such a thing. So even if the grown-up spelling of Macy's hadn't been grandfathered in before the lowercase generation was born, editors would have to decide whether to use the asterisk in place of the star or to treat the star as the stylized apostrophe that it obviously is. I use the word *stylized* a lot in this discussion. To me, the asterisk in the name of the company that wants to be called E*TRADE is a stylized hyphen, the same as the funky old seal in the flag of the Arkansas Democrat-hyphen-Gazette. So when I write about the Internet brokerage, it's *E-Trade*. I maintain that the asterisk is being used as decoration, not punctuation, and should be left out the same way publications leave out the Macy's star and the Democrat-Gazette seal and other symbols that cannot be reproduced. But the asterisk is right there on the keyboard. Some would argue that that is where the line should be drawn, and I can't say that's a wholly unreasonable position.

Toss in Guess(?) and Yahoo(!) and AnnTaylor(.), however, and I think it makes sense to edit out logo punctuation that is either distracting or purely decorative. The false-alarm sentence enders in these logos are bad enough, but the constraints that the question mark and the exclamation point place on headline writers make this decision easy for me. Imagine writing *Earnings Rise at Yahoo!* in 36-point type in a publication that isn't a hired cheerleader for any other company.

I find a certain satisfaction, by the way, in observing that the Web's conventions permit no decorative punctuation in addresses—it's www.yahoo.com and www.etrade.com. Those who lowercase the names of all Web companies should think about this.

"But that's their trademarked name! That's what it says on their press release!" The companies and their trademark lawyers want you to duplicate their capitalization. They also want you to use the trademark symbol. They also want you to use the word *brand* and a generic identifier to guard against the loss of their trademarks (journalists eat Big Macs; McDonald's lawyers might want us to eat BIG MAC®-brand sandwich products). Are you going to give in to all those demands? Do you want your stories to look like press releases?

And don't worry about getting sued over this, unless you're writing ad copy for a competing product. Freedom of the press has weathered far more weighty challenges.

You have to draw the line somewhere. Tomorrow a company could incorporate with the name iNTERNETaBcDe-FgHiJkLmNoPqRsTuVwXyZ.com. Or worse. Are you still going to forsake journalism in favor of logo replication? I hear Kinko's is hiring.

CABINET TITLES

The State Department can be called *State* on second reference, but the leader of the department is *the secretary of state*, not *the secretary of State*. One exception: Because the Treasury gets a capital letter on its own, aside from the Treasury Department, the head of the department is *the secretary of the Treasury*.

SHORTENED FORMS

Retain capitalization of government entities even without the name of the country, state, county or city. The U.S. Postal Service is *the Postal Service*. The Cleveland City Council is *the City Council*. Retain capitalization of shortened forms that are shortened in a very minor way: Dulles International Airport is *Dulles Airport*. When a city name is involved, however, it's better to add *the* and lowercase *airport*: Miami International Airport is *the Miami airport*.

Keep the capital letters, too, if the shortened form simply doesn't work as a common noun. The World Trade Center was a lot of things, but would you call it "a trade center"? I doubt it, and I think references to the Trade Center should be capitalized, to reflect the fact that any such reference is a shortening of the name and not a generic description of the complex's function. Other second-reference truncations look silly either with or without the capitalization. How fearful of "alphabet soup" do you have to be to refer to the Federal Aviation Administration as *the aviation administration*? Is it really an administration? The dictionary might back you up on that, but in the real world it's *the FAA* or *the agency*.

ADJECTIVAL VARIATIONS

Congress, the Bible and *the Constitution* are up, but *congressional, biblical* and *constitutional* are down. Words derived from people's names are an exception, as in *Kafkaesque* and *the Victorian era*.

PLURALS

Lowercase the shared common-noun element in such phrases as *Third and Main streets* and *the Justice and Labor departments*. Retain the capitalization when a title is shared: *Sens. Edward M. Kennedy and Orrin Hatch*; *Presidents George Washington and John Adams*. (Exception: Shared titles that are shared in name only should be lowercased: *presidents George W. Bush and Saddam Hussein.*)

ADJECTIVES DERIVED FROM PROPER NOUNS

Adjectives derived from proper nouns can be close calls, and dictionaries differ, but words such as *balkanization, byzantine, draconian, herculean, lilliputian* and *spartan* should be lowercased in generic references.

WORDS THAT MAKE SENSE ONLY AS PROPER NOUNS

A Boy Scout or a Girl Scout is *a Scout* but not necessarily *a scout*; the word is a reference to the name of the organization, not the ability of the boy or the girl to scout things. *Social Security* is the government benefits program; *social security* is the comfort of having a date lined up for Saturday night. The *Secret Service* protects the president; the *secret service* is a church event you weren't invited to. *Marines* is a closer call; there is a definition of the word that means soldiers of a certain type, but in most references, especially to the U.S. Marine Corps, the word should be capitalized.

When the site of the World Trade Center started being called Ground Zero, purists scoffed at both the term and the capitalization. *Ground zero* means the spot where a nuclear bomb hit, they pointed out. And even if there's no stopping the critical mass behind the term, let's not compound the error by capitalizing it! Ah, but the fact that *Ground Zero* doesn't actually mean *ground zero* is an argument in favor of capitalizing it.

Names are exempt from logic. Lowercase *ground zero* and you're asserting that it's the spot where a nuclear bomb hit; uppercase it and you're simply calling it what it's called.

WHERE THE PROPER ENDS AND THE COMMON BEGINS

In general, signs and phone books and papers of incorporation are good guides to whether a restaurant is *Mom's Restaurant* or simply *Mom's*, to whether a hotel is *the Carlton Hotel* or simply *the Carlton*. With chain establishments, it's best to avoid, or at least avoid capitalizing, the common-noun elements. There's something silly about *Denny's Restaurant* and *Hilton Hotel*.

A tougher call is a straightforwardly named consumer product. The label says *Philadelphia Cream Cheese*, but is *cream cheese* part of the name or just a description of the contents? *Morton Salt* or *Morton salt*? I prefer avoiding unnecessary capitals, but this one is close to a coin flip. Pick a style and stick with it. With more creatively named products, of course, the choice is easy. *Jane's Krazy Mixed-Up Salt* definitely earns its capital *S*.

THE DIVINE

AP calls for lowercasing *he*, *him*, *his* and other pronouns even when they refer to God. (I agree, but I'm a heathen, so what do I know?) Depending on your audience, you may or may not want to follow that advice.

City AND *State*

You find the contradictions in our language charming, right? The city of New York isn't actually called New York City, but we often call it that to distinguish it from the state of New York. And we capitalize *City*. But when we write *New York state*, to distinguish it from the city, most of us don't capitalize *state*. Why? Just because. Maybe the capitalized *State* after the name of a state would suggest the name of a university, or maybe it's just that such *City* forms have attained honorary name status whereas such *state* forms are clearly nothing more than efforts to clarify. We use such constructions as *the state of New York* and *the city of New York* (capitalize *state* and *city* if you like; publications seem to be about evenly split) in references to actions taken by the state and city governments.

WHAT TO ABBREV.?

The Short and Shorter of Truncations,
Acronyms and Initialisms

One word of caution about the use of acronyms is in order. The apparent stranger at a cocktail party who slaps you on the back with a jovial "Where've you been all these years, you old son-of-a-gun?" is a disconcerting chap. You should know him, you think, but you can't place him for the life of you. Strangers like these occasionally grin at readers out of magazine articles and news stories.

—Theodore M. Bernstein

Style on abbreviations varies even more than that on capitalization. Joining a new publication means memorizing a new list of words that are and aren't abbreviated, and how they're abbreviated. And then there are words that can be abbreviated in headlines but not in text.

For those unaccustomed to thinking about style and consistency, one of the hardest things to master about abbreviations is context. In many cases, things that are abbreviated in specific references are spelled out in more general references. In Associated Press style, for example, *Sen.* Barbara Boxer is a *senator*; *Dec. 7* is in *December*; Sheridan, *Wyo.*, is in *Wyoming*; and 223 *S. Sixth St.* is on *South Sixth Street*. Some things are abbreviated as adjectives but not as nouns: Also in AP style, the *U.N.* Security Council is part of the *United Nations*, and *U.S.* residents live in the *United States*.

Abbreviations are generally not used in quotations—it's *Senator Barbara Boxer* unless somebody actually said "Sen"— but there are exceptions there, too. Virtually nobody spells out the *Mr.* in *Mr. Smith*, the *Mrs.* in *Mrs. Jones*, the *Dr.* in *Dr. Kildare* or the *St.* in *St. Louis*, even in a quote.

Newspaper style is generally more abbreviation-happy than style for other publications, though some magazines use abbreviations that few newspapers do. I'm not fond of any of these, but you'll see some magazines use *Mt.* and *Ft.* for *Mount* and *Fort* in place names; *ft.* and *in.* for *feet* and *inches*; *Rm.* and *Ste.* for *room* and *suite* numbers; *lbs.* and *oz.* for *pounds* and *ounces*; *hrs.* and *mins.* for *hours* and *minutes*; and *p.* and *pp.* for page numbers.

STATES AND ADDRESSES

The use of postal abbreviations outside full mailing addresses is a telltale sign of amateurism; few if any big-time publications use them routinely. In fact, any abbreviation at all of the hard-to-abbreviate and short-enough-as-they-are Alaska, Hawaii, Idaho, Iowa, Maine, Ohio or Utah is another dead giveaway. (AP calls for a spelled-out Texas as well, but some reputable publications opt for Tex.) And watch out for the impostors Kans., Nebr., N.Mex., Penna. and Wisc. According to AP style, the state abbreviations, if you're using them with cities, are Ala., Alaska, Ariz., Ark., Calif., Colo., Conn., Del., Fla., Ga., Hawaii, Idaho, Ill., Ind., Iowa, Kan., Ky., La., Maine, Md., Mass., Mich., Minn., Miss., Mo., Mont., Neb.,

Nev., N.H., N.J., N.M., N.Y., N.C., N.D., Ohio, Okla., Ore., Pa., R.I., S.C., S.D., Tenn., Texas, Utah, Vt., Va., Wash., W.Va., Wis. and Wyo.

In AP style compass directions and *Avenue* (*Ave.*), *Boulevard* (*Blvd.*) and *Street* (*St.*) are abbreviated in full street addresses. Wall Street Journal style adds *Road* (*Rd.*). The New York Times and Washington Post stylebooks are oddly vague. The Times abbreviates "*Avenue, Street, Road* and the like" in "headlines, charts, maps, lists and tables, but not in ordinary copy," whatever "and the like" means. The Post stylebook lists what *not* to abbreviate. Note that compass directions aren't always truly compass directions: For example, South Carolina Ave. in Washington, D.C., is named for the state of South Carolina; it isn't the south part of something called Carolina Avenue. So you'd write *123 S. Main St.* but *608 South Carolina Ave. SE.*

NAMES

Names, aside from initials, are virtually never abbreviated. Please, no *Chas.*, *Robt.* or *Wm.*, unless you're writing for the phone book.

CORPORATE IDENTIFIERS

Many publications, including most newspapers, abbreviate such things as *Inc.*, *Co.*, *Corp.* and *Ltd.*, if they use them at all, in company names. The New York Times abbreviates only *Inc.* and its foreign equivalents (including *Ltd.*).

Initial Reactions and Second Thoughts (IRAST)

Sometimes, as I learned at an early age at the kitchen table with Mom, you just have to accept alphabet soup.

The natural instinct of a careful writer or editor is to spell out all initialisms more obscure than, say, *FBI* and *CIA*. In the computer age, however, editors need to rethink this policy. A copy editor I used to work with—an older man—would come across a phrase like *the JPEG format* and say, with a disgusted sigh: "J-P-E-G? I have no idea what that means!"

"Joint Photographic Experts Group," I would reply. "Now do you know what it means?"

The spelled-out version of such an initialism not only adds nothing to a reader's understanding, it actually might introduce confusion. Lots of computer users will recognize a reference to a JPEG, but how many have ever heard of the Joint Photographic Experts Group? Quiz your computer-savvy friends sometime about what *ASCII* or *ISDN* stands for. These initialisms take on a life of their own, and although I think many trends of computerese should be resisted, this isn't one of them.

With borderline cases, in which the spelled-out term actually has some name recognition, and with new terms, I suggest reversing the usual order. If you are going to use an initialism on second reference, you might introduce it in parentheses following the term—*the United Nations High Commissioner for Refugees (UNHCR)*; however, with a technical term better known by its initials it might be better to write the initialism first—*DSL (digital subscriber line) connection*. This acknowledges the prevalence of the abbreviated form, and it also handily skirts a nasty hyphenation issue, as the fastidiously correct form would be *digital-subscriber-line connection*.

Note the lowercase letters. The mere existence of an acronym or initialism has no bearing on whether the spelled-out term is capitalized. *Joint Photographic Experts Group* is a proper noun, but *acquired immune deficiency syndrome* and *individual retirement account* are not.

Acronyms and Initialisms

See Elephant No. 3 for capitalization advice. One other thing: Terms known primarily by their initials in spoken English often get mistranslated when people try to spell them out in writing. ATMs are automated (not automatic) teller machines, HMOs are health-maintenance (not management) organizations, and the DEA is the Drug Enforcement Administration (not Agency).

To *The* or Not to *The*?

True acronyms for organizations and the like get no *the*. It's *the North Atlantic Treaty Organization*, but NATO is simply *NATO*. Initialisms generally get *the* if their spelled-out counterparts do. The Environmental Protection Agency is *the EPA*. No *the*, however, if an initialism is short for an already-short form that has already lost its *the*. Cabinet departments are funny this way: The State Department is often simply called State, and the Department of Health and Human Services can be Health and Human Services, so when you take the latter abbreviation one step further and call the department HHS, you can skip the *the* there too.

Also skip the *the* for initialisms that have supplanted their spelled-out forebears. The American Automobile Association is now simply AAA, the American Association of Retired Persons is now simply AARP and the National Association of Securities Dealers is now simply NASD. I understand *AAA* (it's been known that way for decades) and maybe *AARP* (could half of its members have correctly guessed the spelled-out name?), and I'm rooting for the NAACP to go the initial route (to get rid of the full name's unfortunate *Colored*), but in general I think this non-abbreviation abbreviation trend is ridiculous. The American Electronics Association set my eyes a-rolling by calling for a cute little *e* when it sort of kind of half changed its name to AeA.

DOTS OR NOT?

The use of periods with acronyms and initialisms is, like their capitalization, rather idiosyncratic. In general, periods are uncommon with more than two letters. Associated Press style calls for periods in *U.S.*, *U.N.*, *a.m.*, *p.m.*, *B.C.* and *A.D.* but few others. Washington Post and Wall Street Journal guidelines are similar. New York Times style calls for periods in initialisms (but not acronyms) in which each letter stands for a separate word.

WHICH ONE IS RIGHT AGAIN?

*A Quick Review of Problem Pairs
(and Trios and . . .)*

It's a wise dog that scratches its own fleas.

—William Strunk

It's multiple-choice time. I'm assuming my readers are not absolute beginners, so forgive me if I don't discuss *its* and *it's* beyond the above gem from "The [Other Book] of Style."

A AND *An*

For choosing *a* or *an*, spelling doesn't matter; pronunciation does. *A* is for consonant sounds; *an* is for vowel sounds. The ever-popular *an historic* is incorrect, at least for American speakers, because *historic* does not begin with a vowel sound. Even those Americans who say "an istoric" will admit that they say "historic," with the consonant *h*, when the word stands alone. I don't care whether "an istoric" rolls off your tongue more easily than "a historic"; you don't go altering your pronunciation of a word in order to change the article you use before it. Your comfort is none of the language's concern.

Most of the times I've heard "an historic," however, it has been from blustery types who heartily pronounce the *h*. Think Howard Cosell.

Affect AND *Effect*

To affect is to have an effect on. Remember that *affect* is the verb and *effect* is the noun and you'll almost always be correct. The two exceptions: *Effect* can be a verb that means "to bring about," as in *to effect change*. And *affect* can be a noun that means "emotional state or the outward expression thereof," as in the psychological observation that someone displays *a flat affect*.

Attorney AND *Lawyer*

Lawyer is almost always safe, except when a non-lawyer is acting as his own attorney. *Attorney* means "person representing." So you can be *an attorney for the defendant* or *the defendant's attorney* or *an attorney in the case*, but you can't be *a New York attorney* or *a patent attorney* or *an attorney at the law firm*.

A While AND *Awhile*

Awhile (one word) means "for a while" (three words). *A while* (two words) means "a while" (two words). You can *stay awhile*, or you can *stay for a while*. *For awhile* would mean "for for a while."

Cache AND *Cachet*

A *cache* (pronounced "cash") is a storage place or hiding place or the contents of that place. *Cachet* (pronounced "cash-AY") is a French word meaning "prestige."

Compare to AND *Compare With*

Forget the old axiom that *compare to* is for similarities and *compare with* is for differences. The thing to remember is that *compare to* means *liken to*, period. Comparisons that actually weigh either similarities or differences point by point are comparisons *with*.

Compose, Comprise, Constitute AND THE OTHERS

All of the following are correct:

The Big Ten is made up of 11 universities.

The Big Ten is composed of 11 universities.

The Big Ten consists of 11 universities.

The Big Ten comprises 11 universities.

Eleven universities make up the Big Ten.

Eleven universities constitute the Big Ten.

Convince AND *Persuade*

The general guideline is that you convince someone *of* something or *that* something is true but you persuade someone *to* do something. It is not incorrect, however, to use *persuade* with *of* or *that*, just as a *persuasive* speaker need not inspire action beyond the changing of minds.

Different From AND *Different Than*

Different from is correct when it makes sense to use it. But sometimes it doesn't make sense. Observe: *Clinton is a different man than he was during his presidency.* Nothing wrong with that sentence. It could be *Clinton is a different man from the man he was during his presidency*, but that would be an unnecessary and awkward rewrite.

Different to, by the way, is a British variant.

Due to AND *Because Of*

You may have been taught that *due to* should always be changed to *because of*, but *due to* has its place. If *attributable to* could be substituted, *due to* is fine.

WRONG: *They starved due to the drought.* (They starved *attributable to* the drought? No. They starved *because of* the drought.)

RIGHT: *The famine was due to* (attributable to) *the drought.*

Insure, Ensure AND *Assure*

To make sure that something happens or doesn't happen is to *ensure. Insure* is a variant for that meaning, but careful writers use it only in the sense of insurance policies. You *assure* other people that something will or won't happen.

> *As I left for the post office, I assured my wife that I would ensure that the package was insured.*

Like AND *As*

A song by Tucson's Phantom Limbs, the greatest band you've never heard of, starts like this:

> *We were sitting around like sophomores do, arguing ethics.*

In a rock-'n'-roll song or a conversation, that's good. Grammatical correctness can be dorky at times. If you're writing prose, however, unless you're deliberately going for a casual, break-the-rules effect, the sentence would have to read *as sophomores do.* Or *like sophomores* without the *do. Sophomores* are something we can be like. *Sophomores do* is not something we can be like. We do something *as* sophomores do.

You could argue that truly conversational writing would ignore this distinction, but you'd be pretty lonely. On some usage points, authorities have made peace with the gulf between the spoken word and the written word (see "*Who* and *Whom*" at the end of this Elephant). Nobody ever said English was logical.

Prior to/Following AND *Before/After*

Prior to and *following* aren't wrong, but the less-stilted *before* and *after* are preferred.

That AND *Which*

You've probably heard the difference described in terms of nonrestrictive vs. restrictive clauses or nonessential vs. essential clauses. If you don't quite grasp all that, an easy memory aid is that *which* should be preceded by a comma or a comma equivalent (an open parenthesis or a dash).

WRONG: *Michigan leads Ohio State in the rivalry, a fact which Schembechler is quick to note.*

RIGHT: *Michigan leads Ohio State in the rivalry, a fact that Schembechler is quick to note.*

RIGHT: *The rivalry, which is considered one of college football's most significant, continues to pack stadiums in Ann Arbor and Columbus.*

> **RIGHT:** *A rivalry that is considered one of college football's most significant continues to pack stadiums in Ann Arbor and Columbus.*

Note, however, that occasionally a comma will end up before a *that*:

> **RIGHT:** *The attention the rivalry attracts is sometimes resented at the other teams, including Penn State and Iowa, that make up the Big Ten Conference.*

The Penn State-Iowa clause interrupts a phrase that correctly reads *the other teams that make up the Big Ten Conference*, not *the other teams which make up the Big Ten Conference*.

That AND *Who*

It's usually carelessness, not confusion, that leads to errors such as *the companies who are involved in the venture*. Sometimes, though, it's not clear whether a reference is to an entity or to a person. Does *toymakers* mean toymakers as in Geppetto (*who*) or toymakers such as Mattel (*that*)? When in doubt, go with *that*, as in a reference to toymakers or importers that might include one-person operations as well as multinational corporations.

Who AND *Whom*

I have no passionate feelings about the distinction between *who* and *whom*. Twenty years ago I was ready for *whom* to go away except in the *for whom the bell tolls* sense, but it has stuck around. So here's the standard test:

Look at the clause (not the sentence) in which *who/whom* occurs, turning it around if necessary. If *who/whom* would be replaced by *he, she* or *they*, it's *who*. If it would be replaced by *him, her* or *them*, it's *whom*.

> *I don't know who is going to clean up this mess.* (*He* is going to clean up this mess. Remember: Clause, not sentence, so the test isn't "I don't know *him*.")

> *I don't know whom she told to clean up the mess.* (She told *her* to clean up the mess.)

Grammar isn't always pretty, and idiom tends to butt heads with this rule. *Whom do you trust?* and *Whom will it be?* are technically correct but painfully stilted. Go ahead and use *Who do you trust?* and *Who will it be?* except in the most formal of writing.

LIES YOUR ENGLISH TEACHER TOLD YOU

The Big Myths of English Usage

That is the kind [or type or sort] of nonsense [or insubordination or English or arrant pedantry, or maybe rule or thing] up with which I will not put!

—WINSTON CHURCHILL, MAYBE, TO AN EDITOR
WHO QUESTIONED HIS ENDING A SENTENCE
WITH A PREPOSITION

"Never split an infinitive." "Never end a sentence with a preposition." "Never begin a sentence with a conjunction." "Never use contractions." "Always write in complete sentences." "Never use the passive voice." "Never write in the first person." "Never address the reader directly."

Wrong. Wrong. Wrong. Wrong. Wrong. Wrong. Wrong. Wrong.

THE SPLIT INFINITIVE

Split infinitives are the chicken cacciatore of English usage. If you see a stereotypical fat Italian mamma slaving over a hot stove in a TV commercial, the phrase "My CHICKen CACCiatore!" isn't far behind.

And if you see a schoolmarmish type on TV or at the movies and the talk turns to language, there's a good chance that "split infinitives" will come up. Tell a new acquaintance that you're an editor or an English teacher or a professional writer and the reply might be "I'd better make sure I don't split any infinitives in front of you!"

So, why is splitting an infinitive the cardinal sin of English grammar?

It isn't, any more than chicken cacciatore is the crowning achievement of Italian cooking. I know of no usage authorities who believe that split infinitives are always wrong, but I take a more extreme position than most: More often than not, in my opinion, infinitives are *better* split.

The infinitive is the *to* form of a verb. Foreign-language students will recognize it as the most basic form. Speakers of French use the verb *aller* to express "to go." That infinitive is perhaps the most famously split infinitive in English—"to boldly go where no man has gone before," from the introduction to "Star Trek." A translation into French, of course, would contain no such split, because it's impossible to stick another word in the middle of *aller*. A common explanation of the split-infinitive taboo traces it to grammarians enamored of Latin, another language of single-word infinitives.

Listen to a radio personality who caters to a conservative audience and there's a good chance you'll hear an awkwardly unsplit infinitive. Paul Harvey, for instance, goes out of his way to avoid splits. I once heard him say something like "He went to Wal-Mart personally to thank the employees."

Split infinitives are common for a simple reason: The most natural place to put a modifier is directly before the word or phrase it modifies. So if you have an infinitive and you're looking to use an adverb to modify the verb, the closest location is between the *to* and the verb: *He went to Wal-Mart to personally thank the employees.* The farther away that modifier gets, the greater the chance that a reader will mistakenly interpret it as belonging to a different word or phrase.

But the rabid anti-splitters seem to think there is virtue in the *[blank]ly to [blank]* construction. In the Paul Harvey sentence above, I think the most natural interpretation is that he's saying the man in question went to Wal-Mart personally, as if there's a way to go to a store without going there personally. The funny thing is that the split could have been avoided quite gracefully. Harvey could have said, "He went to Wal-Mart to thank the employees personally."

You won't always find such an easy compromise. Observe: *I need deadline pressure to really do my best work. Really*, which really means "truly" in this somewhat idiomatic usage, is inextricably linked to *do. To do my best work really* makes little sense; if anything, it sounds like a desperate insistence that I'm not lying. *Really to do my best work* is all but gibberish.

Here's another example, from a wire-service article during the run-up to the 2003 war in Iraq:

> *Losses widened on Wall Street after Secretary of State Colin Powell said Iraq failed totally to account for its weapons of mass destruction.*

The meaning, clearly, is that Iraq *failed to totally account for* the weapons. *Totally* modifies the verb phrase *account for*, and the most natural place for the adverb is usually right before the verb. *Failed to account totally for* imposes a much more objectionable split, as *account* makes little sense in this context without *for* immediately afterward. Put *totally* anywhere else and the sentence sounds like the work of a 13-year-old Valley girl ("Iraq, like, *totally* failed to account for the weapons!").

In fairness, here's an example where unsplitting would have been a good idea:

> *Benetton's Sisley line of clothing will contain a Philips Electronics radio-frequency ID tag that will replace bar codes, which have to be manually scanned.*

In this case *split verb* would be a more accurate term than *split infinitive*, because the adverb comes between the helping verb and the verb rather than between *to* and the verb. Opponents of split infinitives tend to extend the concept to split verbs.

But the important lesson of this example is how the ear is more reliable than the rule of thumb. I said before that the best place for an adverb is immediately before the verb it modifies, but notice how in this case such a placement weakens the word that should carry the emphasis. When I say I need deadline pressure to really do my best work, the *do my best work* part is most important; *really* is just along for the ride. When Colin Powell said Iraq failed to totally account for its weapons of mass destruction, *totally* is important, but the accounting-for part is the news. In the Benetton example, however, the *scanned* part is a given. It's a bar code; of course it needs to be scanned. The meat of the sentence is that it has to be scanned *manually*, and that's the most natural way to say it. Writers and editors often make the mistake of thinking earlier is better when it comes to getting something important into a sentence, but the end is often the most powerful place.

Repeat after me: There is nothing inherently wrong with splitting infinitives. If an unsplit version sounds better, use it. If it's a 50-50 shot, as in the Paul Harvey example, go ahead and humor the mythmakers. But don't feel the need, even if the split version sounds only a tiny bit better than an unsplit alternative, to cave in to this so-called rule.

Ending Sentences With Prepositions

A reporter reading over her work after I had edited it was shocked to find the words *the career she went to school for* under her byline.

"I went out of my way to avoid ending that sentence with a preposition!" she said.

"It showed," I said.

As with split infinitives, forget about the alleged ban, but use your ear. I changed *the career for which she went to school*, but I wouldn't change *the city of which he was mayor* to *the city he was mayor of.* The *of which* construction tends to be stilted, but sometimes it's better than the alternative.

Beginning Sentences With Conjunctions

Starting a sentence with a conjunction is a literary device that can be overused. And it can be annoying. But there's nothing inherently evil about it.

Contractions

Unless you're writing an ultraformal academic paper or want to communicate the idea that you're very, very constipated, don't strain to avoid contractions. In other constipation news, if an unscientific sampling of my e-mail inbox is any indication, many people are quite uptight about the fact that *'s* can stand for either *is* or *has*. Unless that dual role could somehow cause confusion, don't worry about it.

COMPLETE SENTENCES

Of all the misconceptions that make up Elephant No. 6, "Always write in complete sentences" comes closest to being a genuine rule. It's a misconception because sentence fragments can be effective if used skillfully, but it's darn close to a rule because writers should master the complete-sentence technique before getting fragment-happy. In other words, if you're an editor and you want to "correct" a fragment, your argument should be "This doesn't work." The correct response to the argument "This is a fragment" is "So what?"

PASSIVE VOICE

The active voice is better when it makes sense to use it. But sometimes it doesn't make sense. Sometimes the person or thing doing the acting is unimportant or even unknown. Observe: *The winning numbers in the $7.4 billion Powerball lottery will be drawn tonight. Louis was born in Detroit. Wilmington-based Delmarva Enterprises Inc. will be sold to a small Japanese manufacturing company.* The last one is a close call, but a Wilmington newspaper would want to lead with the "passive" Wilmington company rather than the "active" buyer.

The First Person

It's often inappropriate to write *I* this and *I* that, but once you decide to be the center of attention, I would rather read *I* than *this writer* or other such silliness.

Addressing the Reader

In a corollary to the *I* thing, one is supposed to avoid referring to one's audience as anything other than *one*. *You* know that's ridiculous, right?

SOME GRAY AREAS

Proceed With Caution

What we require is neither a language that is cramped nor a language gone wild.

—THEODORE M. BERNSTEIN

The following entries apply to "rules" that aren't quite myths but certainly aren't gospel. Many are dueling alternatives without the kind of consensus that would have landed them in Elephant No. 5. Keep in mind that ignoring tradition on some of these points is likely to make people white with rage.

Data AND *Media*

To many, the use of these words in their original plural form is a litmus test for literacy, so it takes some bravery to deviate from the norm. But I think the words are now singular in most cases.

Data was a plural word when its singular form was still alive. When was the last time you saw *datum* anywhere but in a discussion of this issue? The purists are trying to keep the singular form on life support, but I say it's time to pull the plug and acknowledge that *data* is a collective noun, like *information.*

Media is plural when it refers to the plural of *medium*, but as I pointed out in my first book, usually it doesn't. When an artist works in *mixed media*, that's a plural usage. Oil painting is a medium, collage art is a medium, sculpture is a medium.

The news media began as a similar plural term—it referred to print, radio and television. The plural usage still exists, with the online world as another medium, but usually when people refer to *the media* (meaning the news media), they're using it as a collective singular. That singular often overlaps with the print-radio-television-and-Internet plural that I described, but listen more closely and it's clear that those media are not what people have in mind.

Use the "mediums" test: If you can't find a medium in the media that is/are being mentioned, *media* cannot be a plural. ABC, CBS, NBC and Fox are part of the media, but neither ABC nor CBS nor NBC nor Fox is a medium. Peter Jennings, Dan Rather, Tom Brokaw and Brit Hume are part of the media, but not one of them is a medium (though Sam Donaldson might be). Sometimes the issue is a simple question of *is* vs. *are*: Change *The media are restless tonight* to *The media is restless tonight*, because obviously the reference is to the communicators, not the modes of communication. (Can a singular word really represent such a plural idea? Of course: Think of *crowd*, *mob*, *throng*.) If you're not quite brave enough to take such a radical step, of course, you could recast the sentence.

In other cases, recasting is your only option. The plural *media* in *The various media take different approaches* makes sense if those various media are print, radio, television and the Internet, but the sentence is fundamentally flawed if *various media* is supposed to mean the various media outlets or the various media representatives.

Gender

Traditionalists change *gender* to *sex* when it means anything but the labeling of foreign-language nouns as masculine or feminine. Making innocent passages sound racy isn't a bad way to get people's attention, but it's not so good if clarity is your goal. If you haven't noticed, *sex* is busy these days (as evidenced by the popular expression "Let's get busy!"). The "difference between boys and girls" meaning of *gender*, like the emergence of the verb *to host*, is an excellent example of useful linguistic evolution.

Hike

A hike is a walk. A hike is also an increase, whether the one-meaning-per-word contingent likes it or not. The "increase" usage is slangy, to be sure, so I would use it only sparingly, but it's silly to ban such a thing. I would use the inelegant verb form *to hike*, meaning "to increase," even more sparingly. The alternatives include *to increase, to raise, to lift* and *to boost*.

Hopefully AND *More Importantly*

Hopefully, she watched her beloved Yankees try to clinch the pennant.

In a state of being full of hope: That's how *hopefully* is supposed to be used. Heard it used that way much lately? I didn't think so. But using the word the way people use it is widely disparaged.

Smart observers have long pointed out that plenty of *[blank]-ly* adverbs don't strictly mean "in a state of being [blank]." The American Heritage Dictionary and the New York Times stylebook cite *mercifully* and *frankly*. Such "sentence adverbs" apply to a full sentence and not just the nearest word. *Frankly, that guy bugs me* doesn't mean that guy is being frank. *Mercifully, the worst week of my life finally ended* doesn't mean the week was full of mercy.

But another smart observer—Bryan A. Garner, in his book Garner's Modern American Usage—argues that *hopefully* and *thankfully* are traditional adverbs that should be avoided as sentence adverbs, because of their "tarnished history" if nothing else. He makes a good point there. The New York Times stylebook, in cautioning against *hopefully* as a sentence adverb because the usage annoys many readers, has good advice:

With luck, writers and editors will avoid wooden alternatives like it is hoped *or* one hopes.

Interestingly, Garner and the Times trade places on *more importantly*, a less-discussed usage but one that probably has fewer defenders. The Times restates the traditional admonition that the correct phrase is *more important*, because it is short for *what is more important*. Garner points out that *more importantly* often ends up in a position where substituting *what is more important* would make no sense, and he points to *more notably* and *more interestingly* as analogous phrases that work as sentence adverbs. Just plain *importantly*, he adds, also works as a sentence adverb, so why shouldn't *more importantly*?

Host

You can't *host* an event, the purists insist. You *play host to* one. I've been known to resist language evolution (see "e-mail" in the Curmudgeon's Stylebook chapter), but this evolution strikes me as unassailably logical. *Host* started as a noun but is now widely used as a verb. So what? When a simple concept lacks an appropriate verb and a noun is eagerly waiting to fill that role and doesn't sound stupid when it does, so be it.

It isn't hard, especially in advertising copy, to find examples of "verbed" nouns that do sound stupid. Kinko's is "the new way to office"! Do we need a one-word verb meaning "to do office-type stuff"? No, we don't.

Like AND *Such As*

It does feel a bit dorky to keep changing *like* to *such as* when a writer refers to something in the "for example" sense rather than the "resembling" sense, but I keep doing it:

> *What 21st-century baseball needs are players like Babe Ruth.* (The sentence isn't calling for the resurrection of Babe Ruth, so *like* is correct.)

Players such as Babe Ruth changed baseball in the 1920s.
(The sentence means Babe Ruth *and* players like him, not
just players who were like him, so *such as* is correct.)

Many authorities dismiss this distinction. The New York
Times stylebook not only defends the "such as" meaning of
like but essentially prescribes it, calling *such as* "stilted." I agree
that *like* tends to sound less stilted, but it's hard to get past the
fact that I'm not *like* me—I *am* me.

A few other problems:

1. Would the Times argue that "There's no one like you"
   (as the Scorpions sing in a 1980s heavy-metal hit) is
   nonsensical? If *like* can mean *such as*, then *you* can be
   someone like you.

2. Every time a usage distinction is wiped out, writers
   lose the ability to use that nuance. Just how much of a
   loss that is will have to be weighed case by case. When
   it was revealed in 2003 that professional moralizer
   William Bennett was a high-stakes, high-volume
   gambler, Bennett's defenders pointed out that Bennett
   had never specifically sermonized about gambling. I
   thought: He condemned things *like* gambling, if not
   things *such as* gambling.

3. Too often, *like* and even *such as* are what I would call
   cliches of technique. Even when *such as* and *not
   only . . . but also* and *as well as* and *from [blank] . . . to
   [blank]* are used correctly, they can become crutches.
   For instance, instead of *companies like* or *companies such
   as* or *such companies as*, why not *companies including*?
   Isn't that closer to the intended meaning?

Hypercorrection warning: If you do choose to police this distinction, use your head. Remember the example that referred to players *resembling* Babe Ruth but not to the dead man himself. If Florida officials are talking about being prepared for another disaster *like* Hurricane Andrew, don't go changing that to *such as*. Hurricane Andrew has already come and gone, so a disaster *like* it is precisely what they're talking about.

Finally, I let my doctrinaire approach on *like* slide when examples are clearly being offered in a casual sense. If I say Spanish tennis star Juan Carlos Ferrero can be counted on to beat *people like Hicham Arazi and Hyung-Taik Lee* but still has trouble with the top players, I'm dropping a couple of names to be colorful rather than simply writing "journeyman players." *Like*, while not technically correct, is better than *such as* in such a case.

Over/Under AND *More Than/Less Than/Fewer Than*

It's probably hopeless to get this expelled from the list of litmus tests, shibboleths or whatever you call the distinctions that separate us from the bookless savages, but is there really any reason that *over* can't mean *more than* and *under* can't mean *less than*? I have argued that *over* and *under* actually make more sense than *more than* and *less than* when something that is measured in countable units is being discussed in fractions of units, or as more of a mass measurement or a rate:

> *She wants a big family—more than three children.* (Fine. More than three is four or five or six or . . .)

My walk to work every day is more than three miles. (Four miles? Well, no, it's more like 3.1 miles. I call that *over three miles.*)

At the height of the storm, the rainfall accumulated at more than one inch per hour. (Two inches? Well, no, more like 1.3 inches. I call that *over one inch.*)

Even if you're not ready to accept *under* in such instances, it's clear that *less than* makes more sense than *fewer than*. Use *fewer than* for things being counted individually: *Fewer students are taking French this year.*

Persons AND *People*

Some people insist that *persons* is the correct plural of *person* when a definite number is involved. They reserve *people* for fuzzier references:

Of all the people in this room, I can think of two persons who could beat me up.

The spoken word isn't always a good test of correct usage, but I would take a cue from conversational language here. Have you ever known anyone stiff enough to use the word *persons* in conversation?

AGREED?

Making Sure the Parts of Speech Get Along

I is what I is and what I am is like my mamey.

—Missy Misdemeanor Elliott

Singular subjects get singular verbs and pronouns, and plural subjects get plural verbs and pronouns. What could be simpler than that? Now you'll have to excuse me—a bunch of us is going to the mall.

I hope even the most doctrinaire, sentence-diagramming "But that's the *subject*" types are saying "Hold it a minute" at this point. A bunch of us *is* going? Of course not. *A bunch is going*, in a way, but the real meaning of the sentence is that *us*—excuse me, *we*—are going. That's the test to use when the agreement question is a close call.

Bunch really isn't a close call, even though it can take both singular and plural verbs. The answer tends to be clear: *A bunch of parsley* is *required for the recipe*, but *a bunch of us* are *going to the mall.*

Lot is another easy one. A lot in the sense of an auction offering or a piece of real estate is clearly singular. The common expression *a lot of [blank]* depends on whether you're filling in the blank with a mass noun or a count noun. A lot of people *like* ketchup, but a lot of ketchup *goes* to waste.

Such words as *association* and *organization* are concrete singulars. *Number* and *variety* get plural verbs with the indefinite article but singular verbs with the definite article. A *number of people* are *asking me questions, but* the *number of questions* is *surprising.*

Group is the tricky one:

A group of surgeons is calling for new warnings on cigarette packaging. (Are you talking about the group or the surgeons? In this case it's the group.)

A group of surgeons are going to Funnybonz for open-mike night. (Are you talking about the group or the surgeons? In this case it's the surgeons.)

But if you take out the *of surgeons* part, *group* reverts to its natural singular state: *A group is going to Funnybonz.*

Another *group*-like example:

A collection of coins worth more than $1 million is for sale.

A collection of small-time hoodlums are planning to steal the coins.

As you make peace with the idea of a plural verb with a technically singular subject, however, remain on the lookout for the common error of proximity. When a tennis commentator said, "The timing of her strokes are just beautiful," it wasn't for any of the reasons just described; it was a slip of the tongue caused by the proximity of the word *strokes* to the verb. The weatherman's "The next batch of clouds slide through" is a closer call, but with *batch* I'd stick with *slides*. (My favorite error of proximity: For many years, the announcer on "Jeopardy" would announce contestants' money totals—which often ended with an odd single dollar because of Final Jeopardy wagering strategies—as something like "Ten thousand five hundred and one *dollar*.")

Sometimes the decision could be a coin toss. *A series of specials on PBS document(s) the civil-rights movement.* The series documents, and the specials document. Take your pick.

ARE THEY A *They* OR AN *It*?

And now for a brief musical interlude, starring Elvis Costello and the Attractions . . .

> *Oliver's Army is here to stay.*
> *Oliver's Army are on their way.*

Army are? Well, no, at least not in American English. But Costello is British, and *royal* subject-verb agreement assigns plural verbs and pronouns to singular nouns that represent multiple-person groups or institutions.

As odd as it sounds to Americans to hear of what an army *are* doing, this approach does steer clear of some confusion.

In American English, even the simplest, most widely acknowledged application of this principle confuses many writers and editors. The Associated Press Stylebook's entry on *couple* is quite clear and sensible . . .

> *When used in the sense of two people, the word takes plural*
> *verbs and pronouns:* The couple were married Saturday
> and left Sunday on their honeymoon. They will return
> in two weeks. *In the sense of a single unit, use a singular*
> *verb:* Each couple was asked to give $10.

. . . but it confuses the heck out of a lot of newspaper people.

Try to extend the principle any further than *trio* or *three-some* and you're in some muck. Some authorities will tell you that *family* works this way, too, but it's probably better to use *family members* and other tricks to write around the issue.

The growing use of singular nouns as sports-team names has led to an outbreak of British English on U.S. sports pages. Neither alternative is particularly attractive, but it really should be *The Miami Heat wins*, not *The Miami Heat win*.

It's hard to blame the sports-page neo-Brits, given the mismatch between the formal conventions of American English and the way people actually talk. If you ask me about the Washington Capitals and I say, "I really like them," am I saying "them" purely because *Capitals* is a plural noun? I don't think so. Fans of the singularly named Tampa Bay Lightning don't say, "I really like *it*." Ask me about the band R.E.M. and I'll say "them" too. Heck, if you ask me about the selection at Safeway, I'll say "they" have good stuff and bad stuff.

I'm not calling for a revolution in written American English, but I am spotlighting yet another area where some things that are technically correct are better left unwritten. Throw in a reference to *the band members* so you can switch to *them* in an R.E.M. review. Be sure a sentence begins with *The Capitals* instead of *Washington* if it's going to need a *they* later on.

OTHER AGREEMENT ISSUES

Agreement is a huge topic, but the following should cover most of the related issues you'll encounter.

SINGULAR ENTITIES WITH PLURAL NAMES

Unlike musical groups and sports teams, countries, companies and organizations take singular verbs and pronouns even if they're plural. The Beatles *were* greeted enthusiastically on their first trip to the United States, but the United States *was* eager to meet the Beatles. Vandelay Industries *was* supposed to be employing George Costanza. The United Nations *is* regarded as evil in some quarters.

You might think geographical entities would go the country route rather than the band route, but they don't. We say the Allegheny Mountains *are* picturesque and the Hawaiian Islands *are* too.

One of Those

Am I one of those people who writes silly language books? No. I'm one of those people who *write* silly language books. "But, but, but," you might say, "*one . . . writes*." Yes, one writes. But I'm not the only one writing in that sentence. I'm one of *those people who write*. That's the only reason those people are in the sentence. Of those people who write, I am one.

Another example: *Pectin is one of the "cements" that holds plant fibers together.* OK, so the sentence says that (a) pectin is one of the "cements" and (b) pectin holds plant fibers together. What's missing from this equation? The fact that *all* such "cements" hold plant fibers together! The sentence was defining *cements*, not just tossing in a little tidbit about a group that pectin belongs to before going back to talking about what pectin does. Pectin is one of the "cements" that *hold* plant fibers together.

None

Some say *none* means "not one" and therefore takes singular verbs. (AP allows for exceptions only when the singular verb would clearly be wrong: *None of the taxes have been paid.*) Most authorities, however, recognize that *none* often means "not any" and therefore works better with a plural verb. To me, *none is, none has* and the like tend to sound stilted. When either the singular verb or the plural verb would work, I prefer the plural:

> *I know a lot of people in Texas, but none go to monster-truck shows.*

Sometimes the singular verb is clearly the better choice:

> *Of the films to have won Oscars in the past 50 years, none speaks to me as much as "Annie Hall."*

Each

When *each* begins a sentence, follow the singular path: *Each of the beers is good in its own way.* When it follows a plural noun, use the plural: *The beers each have hoppy goodness, a healthy head and a hefty price tag.*

PERCENTAGES, FRACTIONS, PROPORTIONS, AND MASS AND COUNT NOUNS

Go get a drink. Now then . . .

As with *group*, the question of singular vs. plural hinges on the question "What are you talking about?" If you're writing about a certain percentage of working mothers, are you talking about the percentage, or are you talking about the working mothers? Usually it will be the latter, so usually a reference to a percentage will need a plural verb:

RIGHT: *Forty percent of eligible voters are expected to go to the polls.*

AND: *There are 45,000 eligible voters in the county. Forty percent are expected to go to the polls.*

BUT: *Forty percent is considered a poor turnout.*

The idea of mass nouns vs. count nouns is easy (the sandwiches *are* ready, but the soup *is* ready), but sometimes count nouns act like mass nouns. Think of amounts, for example:

> *Two million dollars is going to be spent on the project.*

> *Six months is going to be plenty.*

Dollars and months are simply units of measurement for the mass nouns *time* and *money*, which lord unseen over the sentences.

Sometimes that logic just doesn't yield an acceptable result, and we have to let plurals be plural. Two days *is* a period of time, but *what a difference two days make.*

FALSE SINGULARS

Some words work only in the plural state. A store seeking donations of school supplies for the poor asked listeners in a radio ad to "Donate a school supply." A school supply?

LESS THAN ONE, MORE THAN ZERO

Well-intentioned writers and editors used to equating plural with "more than one" often take a wrong turn when dealing with decimal amounts less than one. What results is such silliness as *Researchers place 0.4 ounce of the liquid on a slide.* Yes, the singular is *one ounce* and 0.4 is less than one, but 0.4 ounces is still *0.4 ounces.* It just is. And if you wanted to talk about zero ounces for some reason, it would be *zero ounces,* not *zero ounce;* the idea of the singular is unique to the number one. Recast as a fraction with the words *of an* if the plural bothers you: *four-tenths of an ounce.*

A WILD PLURAL CHASE

Technically, once you start with a plural your agreement has to stay consistent. So you end up with such following-the-idea-over-a-cliff constructions as *County residents are required to take their cars to authorized service stations for inspections.*

One plural could be changed in this example—*inspection* could mean the idea of inspection rather than *an inspection*—but otherwise you have to acknowledge that there's more than one authorized service station and that county residents don't share a single car. But 21st-century English's lack of a gender-free set of personal pronouns eliminates what once would have been the obvious solution: *Each county resident is required to take his car to an authorized service station for an inspection.* If I were running the language, I would decree that plural pronouns are acceptable in such instances (*Each county resident is required to take their car*), but for the moment many people consider that practice illiterate.

HOLDING OUR BREATHS

Nouns that represent more of an abstract idea than a concrete sense of individual possession can remain singular even with plural possessive pronouns. I can't improve on Theodore Bernstein's examples: *"The fliers plunged to their death. The men earned their living. The three were held prisoner. The spectators held their breath. The depositors' curiosity was piqued."*

COVER YOUR *S*

Possessives and Plurals

The Three Rules for When to Use Apostrophe's:

1. *To Indicate Contractions.*
   Example: "This childbirth really hurt's!"

2. *In Herpetological Phrases.*
   Example: "There's snake's in the Nut 'n' Honey!"

3. *In Letters to Customer Service.*
   Example: "Dear Moron's:"

—Dave Barry

Is it *Jimmy Connors' backhand* or *Jimmy Connors's backhand*? Well, it's the latter in a book or an academic text but probably the former in your local newspaper. The use of an apostrophe alone instead of an apostrophe plus *s* to form the possessive of singular proper nouns ending in *s* is (a) one of the primary differences, along with the general lack of serial commas, en dashes and italics, between newspaper style and formal style, and (b) partly responsible for the widespread confusion about plurals and possessives that Dave Barry mocks.

For singular *common* nouns, by the way, the Associated Press's newspaper style bible calls for *s's* except when the following word begins in *s*: *the hostess's invitation, the hostess' seat.*

PLURALS WITH APOSTROPHES

It's easy to scoff that apostrophes-are-for-possessives-and-not-plurals-you-idiots. If only it were that simple. The use of apostrophes for plurals can be a sign of questionable literacy, but it can also be purely a matter of style. If your publication italicizes individual letters, you can get *A*s on your report card and mind your *p*s and *q*s. But in newspaper style, the plurals of individual letters are made with apostrophes—A's and B's, p's and q's. Otherwise, straight A's would be *straight As*, inviting the question "Straight *as* what?"

Some publications, though not a majority, also routinely use apostrophes for the plurals of "words as words," as in *if's*, *and's* and *but's*. The most notable example is the illogical but widely sanctioned *do's* and *don'ts*, in which one of the words gets an apostrophe to make its plural easier to read while the other word doesn't get an apostrophe because it already has one, albeit for a different reason. I prefer *dos* and *don'ts*, despite the danger that the *dos* part reads like an ancient computer operating system. (Again, italics would solve that problem: *do*s and *don't*s.)

The New York Times complicates matters further by using apostrophes to form the plurals of abbreviations, acronyms, initialisms and numbers. The Times does this in its all-caps headlines for readability, and then in its regular text for consistency with those headlines. So you'll read about *M.D.'s*, *TV's*, *747's* and *the 1950's*. Most other newspapers, by the way, use *1950s* and abbreviate it as *'50s*, with the apostrophe indicating dropped characters. The Times skips the apostrophe of omission, figuring that one apostrophe is plenty in *50's*. (More formal publications might use *fifties* or *Fifties*.)

APOSTROPHE OR APOSTROPHE-*S*?

The New York Times is also one of the few newspapers (the Washington Post is another) to take the formal route on the *s's* question: In the Times and the Post, it's *Jimmy Connors's backhand* and *Burt Reynolds's movies* (and *the hostess's seat*). You'll be stunned to learn that even that simple principle gets mucked up. Stylebooks that call for the formal *s's* tend to follow that with a big *but*. The Chicago Manual of Style makes exceptions for *Jesus'*, *Moses'* and "names of more than one syllable with an unaccented ending pronounced *eez*." Words Into Type calls for the apostrophe alone "wherever the apostrophe and *s* would make the word difficult to pronounce, as when a sibilant occurs before the last syllable." It adds *Isis'* to the *Jesus'-Moses'-Xerxes'* list. The New York Times mentions "ancient classical" names plus words that end in "two sibilant sounds (*ch*, *j*, *s*, *sh* or *z*) separated only by a vowel sound." It gives *Kansas' climate* and *the sizes' range* as examples, although *sizes* would seem to fall under the guidelines for plurals. The Wall Street Journal: "ancient classical names" and "names of more than one syllable when the last syllable starts as well as ends with an *s* or *s* sound and when that last syllable is unaccented: *Kansas' law*, *Moses' journey*, *Jesus' teachings*, *Texas' cowboys*." The Washington Post: "proper names of more than one syllable ending in *-es*" and "words ending in a silent *s*." So it would be *Arkansas's and Kansas' laws* in the Times and the Journal but *Arkansas' and Kansas's laws* in the Post. I think. (My head hurts.)

THE STATE OF THE STATES

Chicago Manual	Kansas's	Texas's	Arkansas's
Words Into Type	Kansas'	Texas'	Arkansas'
Associated Press	Kansas'	Texas'	Arkansas'
New York Times	Kansas'	Texas'	Arkansas's
Wall Street Journal	Kansas'	Texas'	Arkansas's
Washington Post	Kansas's	Texas's	Arkansas'

Frankly, for Jesus's sake, I don't see what would be so horrible about applying the *s's* principle to all of the names. *Arkansas's* and *Kansas's* and *Texas's* are clearly correct if your style is *Reynolds's* and *Connors's*.

But even I can't give you an exception-free list. Pretty much all stylebooks wisely make pronunciation-driven exceptions for *appearance' sake, conscience' sake* and *goodness' sake*. The Post, especially wisely, adds *Red Sox'* and *White Sox'*, recognizing the plural nature of the creatively spelled names.

PLURAL POSSESSIVES

Remember that the *s's* principle is for *singular* nouns ending in *s*. Plurals ending in *s* get the apostrophe alone when they become possessive, no matter whose style you're using: *the justices' opinion*. Countries, companies and organizations that are plural in form but singular in practice also get the apostrophe alone: *the United States' wealth, Goodwill Industries' work*.

Tricky Plurals

The plural of nouns ending in *s, x* or *z* is generally formed by adding *-es*. This applies even to people's last names, no matter how many times you've heard about inviting "the Jenkins" over for dinner or seen mailboxes labeled "The Atkins'" or even "The Atkin's." (Bruce Jenkins is *Jenkins*. Bruce and Cindy Jenkins are more than one Jenkins, so they're *the Jenkinses*. Who the heck would "the Jenkins" be? Don't let that *s* distract you: You wouldn't refer to Don and Cathy Smith as "the Smith"!)

If a possessive popped up, you would invite the apostrophe along: You might refer to the Jenkinses' place as the *Jenkinses'* for short. If the Jenkinses have more than one Ford, they have Fords; if they have more than one Mercedes, they have Mercedeses (or, in the hands of a facile editor, Mercedes-Benzes).

When the Singular Is Also the Plural

Some words are the same whether singular or plural: *chassis, faux pas, series, species*. More than one McDonald's, likewise, would simply be *McDonald's*, but it's better to avoid such a usage by making it *McDonald's restaurants* or *McDonald's locations*.

The existence of an exception for *series* and the others, of course, only adds to the confusion. And just as people tend to think words ending in *s* are already plural and don't require pluralization, they tend to make those words possessive more readily than they would words ending in other letters. A magnetic attraction develops between the *s* and the apostrophe.

Sportswriters give us *Los Angeles Lakers' center Shaquille O'Neal* when they would never write *Orlando Magic's forward Tracy McGrady*. Again, ignore the *s*. The *Lakers* in *Lakers center* is a simple adjective, just like the *Magic* in *Magic forward*. No apostrophe. Business writers also get flummoxed by the *s*. They'll write *Ford stock rose*, but the same construction suddenly becomes possessive in *General Motors' stock rose*.

Keep the likes of Ford and the Magic in mind when you're wrestling with the likes of General Motors and the Lakers. When you're confused about whether you're dealing with a possessive, substitute a name that doesn't end in *s* and you'll see just how elementary this is.

Possessives are appropriate with apposition. Apposition occurs when you describe something, comma, and then name it, comma. The use of *the* is often an indicator that apposition is taking place. No possessive: *Redskins quarterback Patrick Ramsey is injured*. Yes possessive: *The Redskins' quarterback, Patrick Ramsey, is injured*.

Be aware, though, that apposition and its commas introduce a complication that the simple adjectival label does not. If you've been with me for discussions of *that* vs. *which*, you've heard about restrictive and nonrestrictive, or essential and nonessential, clauses. Commas and apposition are used with nonrestrictive (nonessential) clauses, which are so named because what is between the commas does not restrict, and is not essential to, the meaning of the sentence. So the movie "Rocky" is simply *the movie "Rocky,"* no comma, because "Rocky" is essential to the meaning. Take it out and a reader would be asking, "Movie? What movie?" If the movie in question had come up earlier, however, the comma would be appropriate: *A low-budget underdog of a movie made Sylvester Stallone a household name in the mid-'70s. The movie, "Rocky," won the Oscar for best picture of 1976.* The sentence makes sense even without the name of the movie, so that clause is nonessential and requires commas.

Getting back to the sports examples, apposition is often inappropriate. Basketball players rotate in and out of games, so *the Lakers' center, Shaquille O'Neal,* would work only in a discussion of a specific moment in a game, when he was *the* center. *The Redskins' quarterback, Patrick Ramsey*, is a borderline case. Football teams have more than one quarterback, just as basketball teams have more than one center, but they usually use only one quarterback per game. *Quarterback* can be read to imply *starting quarterback*, so you could get away with Ramsey's commas, even if they're not strictly correct, as long as he's the starter.

In headlines, where the context is less clear and the *the* would usually be dropped, the difference between the label and the possessive is more subtle. The following examples are not as football-specific as they may seem:

Redskins Quarterback Injured

This headline is correct without the apostrophe whether it refers to the starting quarterback or a backup, but readers would assume it's the starter. An apostrophe would be acceptable to hammer home the point that it's the starter:

Redskins' Starting Quarterback Injured

He's *the* starting quarterback, so inserting the apostrophe is appropriate.

Redskins Backup Quarterback Injured

Use an apostrophe only if there's just one backup quarterback.

Redskins Victory Predicted

No apostrophe if there's no victory yet. Yes apostrophe if there was a victory and this is a headline pointing out that the victory *was* predicted beforehand.

> *Redskins' Victory Is Sweet*

It wouldn't be *wrong* without the apostrophe, but the apostrophe is advisable. It's *the Redskins' victory*, not just *a Redskins victory*.

> *Redskins' Fourth Super Bowl Victory Is Sweet*

In this case, *Redskins'* is clearly possessive. The apostrophe is required.

> *Cisco Systems' Stock Falls*

As we leave the football stadium, here's one that's a coin toss. Would you say *Cisco Stock Falls* or *Cisco's Stock Falls*? Either sounds good to me, so *Systems* can go with or without the apostrophe.

Other Issues

The opportunities for confusion when the apostrophe and the *s* are involved never seem to end.

Each Other's, One Another's

Watch the placement of the apostrophe in *each other's* and *one another's*. Never write *each others'* or *one anothers'*. The *other* in these phrases is inherently singular.

Children's

Always use *children's*, never *childrens'*. One is a child; two or more are children. What would *childrens* be?

People's

Like *children*, *people* is already plural, so the possessive form is *people's*, at least in most cases. *Peoples* is correct, however, as the plural of *a people*, as in *the indigenous peoples' religions*.

Doctor's Offices, Driver's Licenses AND Traveler's Checks

Some terms keep their singular possessives even when they become plural. But pluralize as usual if context divorces the pairs:

> *Police searched the hospital, including the doctors' offices.*
>
> *All of the drivers' licenses were confiscated.*
>
> *The travelers' checks were stolen.*

SINGULAR IDEAS IN PLURAL FORM

Politics *is* a fascinating subject. Communications *is* a silly thing to major in. But the plural nature of such singular words does assert itself in some cases:

> *Communications between the two sides have been contentious.*
>
> *My politics are my own business.*

POSSESSIVES AS ANTECEDENTS

In general, if you want to refer back to a noun, you have to present that noun clearly, in unadorned form:

> *Toni Morrison is my favorite novelist. She's fantastic.*

One exception allowed by right-thinking grammarians is that a possessive pronoun may have a possessive antecedent:

> *Toni Morrison's genius is in her ability to create novels that arise from and express the injustices African-Americans have endured.*

That example is a rewrite of a sentence that high-school juniors were asked about on the PSAT, a standardized test. The actual sentence, in which the antecedent was possessive but the pronoun was not, was considered correct by the Educational Testing Service but disputed by a high-school teacher:

> *Toni Morrison's genius enables her to create novels that arise from and express the injustices African-Americans have endured.*

To those who live by the words *no possessive antecedents*, the sentence does contain an error. *Her* is supposed to refer to Toni Morrison, but there is no *Toni Morrison* in the sentence; there is only a *Toni Morrison's*. Enough people subscribe to that notion to make the teacher's point valid: The testing service should have accepted either answer or thrown out the question.

Realistically, I say, the sentence is fine. It's not awkward, and there's no doubt what it means. Set aside my rewrite above, which changes the meaning slightly, and ask yourself how the sentence would have to read to satisfy the technical objection. Maybe:

> *Toni Morrison's genius enables Morrison to create novels that arise from and express the injustices African-Americans have endured.*

A normal person would ask: Why are you repeating *Morrison*?

The kind of person who would insist on the rewrite in the first place would ask: Who's Morrison? There's no Morrison in the sentence; there's only a *Morrison's*. If the possessive can't be an antecedent, how can it be a first reference?

How about:

> *Toni Morrison's genius enables the writer to create novels that arise from and express the injustices African-Americans have endured.*

That one reads nicely, but the technical objection would remain. *Toni Morrison's* can't be a writer. Consider that the "rule" would forbid the following sentence and you'll see why it's untenable:

> *Toni Morrison's feet are killing her.*

Here's the kind of sentence that the prohibition on possessives as antecedents was meant to protect us from:

> *She said she prefers to read novels such as Toni Morrison's, whom she called a genius.*

Teachers Union, *Citizens Group*, ETC.

Some stylebooks call for no apostrophe in formations such as *teachers union*, pointing out that a teachers union is a union *of* teachers more than it is a union *belonging to* teachers.

On the other hand, it is *their* union. That's possessive, right?

On the other other hand, it seems that a truly possessive form would be pronounced differently. *The teachers' union* would be "the teachers' U-nion," not, as the phrase is actually pronounced, "the TEACH-ers union."

On the other other other hand, the apostrophe cannot always be omitted. You can get away with *citizens group* but not *mens group* or *womens group* or *childrens group* (or, to follow the other fork in that road, *men group* or *women group* or *children group*).

So take a close look at your four hands, and take your pick.

THE ANTIQUES PLURAL

Finally, yes, it's *attorneys general*, not *attorney generals*. And *sergeants major* and *courts-martial* (and *pains in the ass*). I think people should know the correct plurals, but I'm afraid I can't join my fellow language buffs in getting all excited about the issue. If I ever become Miss America, the preservation of backward terminology won't be part of my "platform." If *attorney generals* is the worst error you ever commit, you're a genius. (If you do it on purpose, you're a visionary.) The Onion came up with a terrific tweak on the topic: "William Safire Orders Two Whoppers Junior."

A Number of
Problems

Counting on 100 Percent Correctness

Math is hard.

—Barbie

To see how widely divergent style rulings on numbers can be, all you have to do is count to 10. Or ten. Newspapers spell out *one* through *nine* (with 1,001 exceptions) and use numerals starting at 10, but publications that adhere to the more formal Chicago manual don't go to numerals until 101.

If a number begins a sentence, of course, you'll have to spell it out even in newspaper style. Don't forget that all those *and*s we use in conversation are technically incorrect: A sentence about Hank Aaron and Babe Ruth might begin with *Seven hundred fifteen home runs* (it's not *Seven hundred and fifteen*). Quotes, by the way, need not spell out numbers that otherwise wouldn't be spelled out, because there's no pronuncia-tion difference between, say, *78* and *seventy-eight*.

Numbers above 999 get commas, unless they are years. *I made 2,001 mistakes in 2001.*

NUMBER OR NUMERAL?

Stylebooks tend to drone on about obvious exceptions to the general rules about numbers vs. numerals. If Oldsmobile calls its car (or is it a boat?) the Ninety-Eight, you know not to call it the 98, right? Here's a selective list of cases where the answer may not be obvious:

WHAT THE NEW YORK TIMES STYLEBOOK CALLS "NUMBERED EXPRESSIONS"

Use numerals for numbered expressions:

No. 1, Chapter 2, Page 3, Room 4, Act 5, size 6

MONEY

Obviously you want a numeral with a dollar sign: *$6*. But this principle applies in many publications even when the unit of currency is spelled out: *1 euro, 2 cents, 3 pesos*. (In American English, by the way, it's best to avoid currency symbols other than the dollar sign. The cents sign is inelegant, and the symbols for the euro, the British pound and other foreign currencies are unfamiliar to many Americans.)

Conversational expressions, of course, need not play by those rules: *My two cents? I wouldn't do it for a million bucks.*

Millions, Billions and Beyond

Many publications use *1 million*, not *one million*. That starts to look odd in dollar amounts (*$1 million?* One dollar million?), but *$1,000,000* isn't much of an alternative. Such dollar amounts are generally granted an exemption from compound-modifier hyphenation (*a $1 million ransom*, not *a $1-million ransom*), though the hyphen should be used if the dollar amount is part of a larger phrase that contains a hyphen (*$1-million-plus ransom*). Similarly: *1.2-million-member group*.

Percentages

Use *2 percent*, not *two percent*. Percentages, like millions and billions and the like, are usually considered exempt from compound-modifier hyphenation, with the same two-hyphen caveat: *a 45 percent turnout*, *a 45-percent-plus turnout*. The Wall Street Journal avoids the number-vs.-numeral issue and the hyphenation issue (and saves space) by using the percent sign: *a 45% turnout*. I think that's a good idea; the percent sign is just as recognizable as the dollar sign.

Ages

Human ages expressed in years are generally numerals: *They have a 5-year-old daughter and a son who's 4.* Many stylebooks also call for numerals for animals' ages but spell out such things as *a six-year-old building.* Publications vary on whether a baby would be *six months old* or *6 months old*, but I think it's better to spell out such numbers to underscore the special status accorded to years in expressions of age ("I'm 8!" requires no elaboration).

VOTES AND SCORES

Use numerals to express the number of votes in an election or the score in a competition:

The Capitals led 6–1 before the Red Wings pulled out a 7–6 overtime victory.

Early results from Dixville Notch, N.H., showed Chelsea Clinton leading Jenna Bush by 5 votes to 4.

RATIOS AND ODDS

Use numerals to express ratios and the odds for or against an event:

I'll give you 2 to 1 that at least 3 out of 4 people at the poker table will be wearing baseball caps.

MEASUREMENTS

Use numerals for measurements:

He's 6 feet tall.

They pulled out a 2-inch splinter.

It's 3 degrees below zero outside.

I'm going to gain 9 pounds a day if Ben and Jerry stay in business.

Deciding exactly what qualifies as a measurement, though, isn't as easy as it sounds. AP style calls for numerals for dimensions, but what about acres? An acre isn't really a dimension; it's the product of two dimensions. It's probably safe to use the numeral when it's a measurement, but what about *I planted two acres last week*? Farmer types might talk of acres as individual units; planting two acres is a count of how many of these units were planted, not a mathematical measurement that just happened to yield 2.0 acres after multiplication. Along the same lines, you might buy *two gallons* of milk, as in "How many jugs did you buy?," but drink *2 gallons* of milk, as in "How much did you drink?"

A small municipality might measure *2 miles by 1 mile*, but your house would be *three miles away*. The first example involves size; the second tells distance.

By the way, here's how style on height works: Use *feet* with a fully spelled-out expression that includes the word *tall*: *He's 6 feet 1 inch tall. She's 5 feet 2 inches tall.* Use *foot* with shorthand expressions that include hyphens: *He's 6-foot-1. She's 5-foot-2. The basketball team has a 7-foot center.*

DECIMALS AND FRACTIONS

Expressions with decimals are obvious. You need *5* and *1*, not *five* and *one*, to write *5.1*. Fractions that include a whole number should be expressed with numerals and fraction symbols when possible: *He was making 1½ times his old salary.* If a symbol isn't available, follow the whole number with a space and then the numerator and denominator separated by a slash: *The hole had to be 5 11/16 inches in diameter.* Spell things out as necessary if a fractional number starts a sentence: *Three and three-sixteenths was the measurement she kept repeating as she headed to the Home Depot.* But use the conversational *a half* rather than the stilted *one-half* in most cases: *Five and a half pounds is a lot to gain in one day.*

Fractions without whole numbers should be written out, even in references to size: *The handheld computer is five-eighths of an inch thick.*

TIME AND DATE

Numerals are appropriate to express a time whether it's *3:30 p.m.* or *half past 3 o'clock.* Use a simple *3* rather than *3:00*, and avoid the redundant *3 p.m. in the afternoon.* Midnight and noon are *midnight* and *noon*; don't call either of them *12.* If you're programming your VCR, noon is 12 p.m. and midnight is 12 a.m., but I refuse to be drawn into any conversation over whether such designations are truly correct. For the record, though, midnight is the end of a day, not the beginning.

Dates also take numerals. Strunk and White argued for the *7 December 1941* form, but *Dec. 7, 1941*, remains the standard form in American English (note that the trailing comma is needed to set off the year if the sentence continues). Use *7th* (not *Seventh*) in a quote if that's what the person said. (Also, spell out the *December* part unless the person actually said "dess.")

DECADES, AGES AND OTHER INCREMENTS OF 10

Some publications spell out references to other increments of 10, including age ranges, to distinguish them from references to decades: *He was in his sixties during the '60s. Tomorrow's high temperature is expected to be in the upper sixties.*

Notches

Don't extrapolate from the preceding exceptions so that anything remotely related to what we're talking about becomes a numeral. A girl turns *3* on her *third* birthday. An increase from *6* percent to *7* percent is an increase of *one* percentage point. A *12-3* vote is a margin of *nine* votes. If you read Page *11* through Page *15*, you've read *five* pages. A baby who was born at *6* pounds but has grown to *8* pounds has gained *two* pounds.

Consistency

Perfect consistency is impossible. The "Number or Numeral?" discussion is about drawing arbitrary lines. You have to choose which kind of consistency you want to strive for. Do you want *nine* to be *nine* whenever it doesn't fall under one of the exceptions, or do you want to use numerals in every instance to keep things uniform in a sentence in which several numbers will be numerals (*The contest winner ate 11 Big Macs, 10 Quarter Pounders and 9 double cheeseburgers*)? Many stylebooks call for such proximity-related departures from style, but I would stick with *11 Big Macs, 10 Quarter Pounders* and *nine double cheeseburgers*. As I said, you're doomed to inconsistency either way.

The Problems Multiply

Some other sticky issues in the numbers game:

PERCENTAGES AND PERCENTAGE POINTS

If ePruneJuice.com's share of the online prune-juice market was 25 percent last year and is 50 percent this year, how much did it rise? Many writers get distracted by the presence of percentages and say 25 percent. The answer, of course, is 25 percentage points, or 100 percent (the change, 25, is 100 percent of the old number, 25).

Up to 50 Percent or More

You see the pairing of *up to* and *or more* mostly in advertising, but it also comes up in actual writing. Up to 50? That could be as little as zero. Or more? That could be infinitely more. The phrase is meaningless.

The concept of "as little as" or "as much as" is often abused in a more subtle way. How is *as much as 8 to 10 inches of snow* different from *as much as 10 inches*? How is *as early as Tuesday or Wednesday* different from *as early as Tuesday*? When you specify a minimum or a maximum, you're specifying a minimum or a maximum. If you want to be wishy-washy, there are other ways of writing such things.

AVERAGES AND MEDIANS

To get an average, add a list of numbers and divide the result by the number of items in the list. To get a median, take the number in the middle—the number with an equal number of entries higher and lower. Sometimes this distinction doesn't make much of a difference, but often it makes a huge difference. If I tell you a sweatshop pays an average salary of $210,000, that may sound pretty good. But that number could mean there's a $1-million-a-year mogul overseeing four work-ers making $20,000, $15,000, $10,000 and $5,000. The *median* salary is $15,000, whether the top salary is $1 million or $21,000. This is an extreme example, but note how each conclusion is misleading in its own way.

SQUARE DEALS

I had a heck of a time not too long ago convincing a reporter that *100 square miles offshore* made no sense. A square mile is a unit of area, not a linear measure. Something can't be a square mile away from something else any more than you can go out and walk two acres.

In coverage of the Columbia disaster, I caught a copy editor changing a reference to the space shuttle's heat tiles from "6 inches square" to "6 square inches." Uh-uh. The expression may sound colloquial, but *6 inches square* is a legit-imate way of saying something is 6 by 6. For the record, that's 36 square inches.

THE AVERAGE PERSON

The idiom is understandable enough, I suppose, but elegant writers and careful editors know there's no "average" person or employee or house or whatever. The average applies to the number itself, so make it *Physicians in the United States earn an average of $200,000 a year*, not *The average U.S. physician earns $200,000 a year*.

MILLIONS AND BILLIONS

Always, *always* check million and billion numbers; those *m*'s and *b*'s often get mixed up. It is a very common mistake. And if you're dealing with international sources or writers or readers, keep in mind that billions, trillions, etc., mean different things to Americans than they do to people in some other countries, most notably Britain. An American billion is a thousand millions, an American trillion is a thousand billions and so on. In the British system, a billion is a million millions and a trillion is a million billions. Our billion is the British *milliard*. I have no brilliant solution for this potential ambiguity, but do keep it in mind.

BUSINESS-PAGE STAPLES

A company's profit rose 20 percent in the most recent quarter. That means it was 20 percent higher than in the previous quarter, right? Nope. It almost always means compared with the same quarter of the previous fiscal year. That way the comparison isn't skewed by seasonal fluctuations. It'd be nice if stories made that clear, wouldn't it?

And what does *a $10 billion industry* mean? I doubt that most readers know. Before I started working on business copy, I thought it meant it would cost $10 billion to buy up all the companies in that industry. What it means is that the companies in that industry have combined annual revenue of $10 billion. Or at least they did in the most recent year for which figures are available. And that's revenue as in *sales*, meaning income before taxes and other expenses, as opposed to *net income*, which is also known as *earnings* or *profit*. Get the feeling this subject could be a chapter in itself?

Two Dollars to Three Million Dollars?

In speech, it's clear that *two to three million dollars* means $2 million to $3 million. Both *million* and *dollars* are obviously common elements, and if you meant *two dollars to three million dollars*, that's what you'd have said. In writing, however, at least if you're using the common *$2 million* style convention, attempts to reproduce that conversational brevity lead to unintended mirth, if not ambiguity: *$2* means $2, and *$2 to $3 million* means two dollars to three million dollars. Write *$2 million to $3 million* if that's what you mean.

Associated Press style calls for similar caution with percentages—*2 percent to 3 percent* rather than *2 to 3 percent*—but I think the extra *percent* can be dropped unless there's a chance that the first number can be read as something other than a percentage. Write *2 percent to 3 percent of the protesters* to be safe (someone could conceivably think for a second that the first number refers to two protesters), but feel free to write *2 to 3 percent of the oil* (there cannot be "two of the oil").

Dollars Dollars

Use the dollar sign or the word *dollars* but not both: The *$3 dollars* (or even *$3 bucks*) error is common, and it's easy to miss.

Between Is to *And* as *From* Is to *To*

Use *from 300 to 400* or *between 300 and 400* (with the caveats in the next paragraph), not *between 300 to 400*. A hyphen (or en dash, depending on your style) is fine in tabular matter or sometimes for date ranges, but don't mix the shortcut with actual prose. *His 1815-1831 reign* is fine, but *He reigned from 1815-1831* is not.

The *between* approach should be used advisedly, as some people believe it is not inherently exclusive. *Between $500 billion and $600 billion* is safe; it's obviously a rough estimate, and even if it truly means "from $500,000,000,000.01 to $599,999,999,999.99," chances are that won't be an issue. But *between 1999 and 2000* is best avoided. What, it may be sensibly asked, came between 1999 and 2000?

To, by the way, doesn't always require a *from*. *A snowfall of 13 to 15 inches* is smooth and pristine; *a snowfall of from 13 to 15 inches* is marred by the dirty footprints of a clumsy editor.

In financial writing, the from-to sequence is often reversed to emphasize the present or the recent over the more distant: *The company's revenue rose to $15 million from $13 million*. Use commas to avoid ambiguity:

> *Profit rose to $250,000, from $100,000 in the previous year.* (Without the comma, the sentence could be read as meaning the rise occurred in the previous year.)

> *Ford stock rose $1.25, to $13.50.* (Without the comma, *$1.25 to $13.50* could appear to be a range.)

The to-from style is fine for financial writing, but in more general contexts the from-to method is usually a better choice: *He went from 235 pounds to 185.*

A 50-PERCENT-ASSED SOLUTION

In an article packed with precise statistics, go ahead and use *50 percent* next to *49 percent* and *51 percent*. In most cases, however, *half* is a beautiful thing. The use of *50 percent* and

25 percent in imprecise references is especially silly. If you mean about half or about a quarter, say it.

Times More

Times goes with *as much as*. *More* goes with percentage increases. We say *twice as much*, not *two times more*, and the same principle applies, no matter how many times you're multiplying. Some would write off the *times more* usage as idiom, but that ignores a factual problem: Think of what *one time more* would mean and you'll see that *two times more* would actually mean "three times as much as."

Even worse is *times less*. One time less equals zero, so how can a currency be worth five times less than it used to be worth? Multiplication comparisons are not reversible: If the former value is five times the current value, the currency is worth one-fifth as much, or 80 percent less.

OUT OF THE *-fold*

Is *a threefold increase* a tripling (the *result* is three times the starting number) or a quadrupling (the *increase* is three times the starting number)? If you have to stop and think about this one, imagine what a typical reader might be going through. The *-fold* device is best avoided.

FALSE SPECIFICITY

False specificity is a tricky sin to spot, because it's often disguised as non-specificity. Your antennae should go up when you read about, for instance, a credit-card fee that *can vary from 2 percent to 5 percent of the cash advance.* Ah, so it's never 1.9 percent? It's never 6 percent? It's never, uh, zero? If you're going to fudge, learn how to fudge correctly.

Since

After boxer Roy Jones Jr. won a version of the heavyweight championship at 193 pounds in 2003, one major newspaper called him "the lightest heavyweight champion since 205-pound Michael Spinks in the mid-1980s." I guess that's literally true, but then he'd also be the lightest heavyweight champion since 250-pound Lennox Lewis. The *[blank]est since* expression is supposed to point to the last occasion when the notable accomplishment you're referring to was surpassed, and in fact the last person lighter than Jones to win a heavyweight title was Floyd Patterson (182 pounds) in 1956, which makes the point more impressively anyway.

ROUNDING

Fractions lower than half get rounded down; half or more gets rounded up. So 4.44 million becomes 4.4 million if you round numbers in the millions to one decimal place, but 4.45 million becomes 4.5 million. Be careful when rounding a number that has already been rounded: If that 4.5 million that started out as 4.45 million needed to be rounded to a whole number, 5 million would appear to be the correct choice (4.5 rounds up to 5), but it would be wrong, because the raw number, 4.45, rounds down to 4. Also, make sure to use raw numbers to figure percentage changes; rounding can skew the math.

It's a good idea to establish a consistent style on rounding and decimals. Many publications use one decimal place for millions, two for billions, and so on. One decimal place is a good guideline for percentages. But reserve the right to use as many decimal places as necessary when discussing minute but important differences. And remember that *nothing* rounds down to zero. If the Dow Jones Industrial Average rises 0.01 percent, it rose 0.01 percent.

HIGH-RANKING AND LOW-RANKING

The number 1 is a low number, but it's as high a ranking as rankings get. Don't make the amateur-sportswriter error of equating the two *high*s: If Andre Agassi's opponent is ranked 268th in the world, that's a comparatively *low* ranking.

THE LAW OF AVERAGES

There is no "law of averages." If a tossed coin has landed heads up 999 times in a row, neither the "tails is due" fallacy nor the "heads is on a roll" fallacy can be used to predict the outcome of the 1,000th toss. Other factors come into play when writers use this "law" to predict movements in, say, the Dow Jones Industrial Average, but "the law of averages" will never be part of a valid argument.

THE ADVENTURES OF CURLY AND STITCH

The Comma, the Hyphen, the Headaches

If you take hyphens seriously, you will surely go mad.

—John Benbow

Gather half a dozen of the world's best English-language writers and editors, and ask them to look over a page of text. One or two might miss one or two typos, but eventually if they keep passing the page around, everybody will agree that everything's right, right? Well, probably not, if commas or hyphens are involved.

Curly the Comma and Stitch the Hyphen are the black sheep of the English-language family, and it seems that no two people can agree on what to do about them. When a short introductory clause comes up, Curly's ready to do his part, but he's never sure whether he's wanted. Stitch feels the same way about compound modifiers.

MEET CURLY

Curly got off on the wrong foot with English teachers right away, and I can't say he wasn't at fault. The "comma splice" occurs when two sentences are joined with nothing more than a comma: *I like Mike Tyson, I think he would have knocked out Ali.* I doubt that anyone reading this book would be likely to commit a comma splice, but just for the record, here are the basic ways to repair one:

1. Make each sentence a sentence: *I like Mike Tyson. I think he would have knocked out Ali.*
2. Make the comma a semicolon. The semicolon was born to join two sentences single-handedly: *I like Mike Tyson; I think he would have knocked out Ali.*
3. Throw in an *and*. Comma plus *and* equals semicolon: *I like Mike Tyson, and I think he would have knocked out Ali.* If the subject is the same on both sides of the comma splice, as it is in this example, you can replace the comma and the repeated subject with a simple *and*: *I like Mike Tyson and think he would have knocked out Ali.*

Some writers and editors were taught an arbitrary cutoff point at which short introductory clauses are followed by commas, perhaps two or three words. While it's true that the length of such a clause is one criterion for deciding on comma or no comma, other criteria are more important:

- **Clarity.** Often you don't need a comma with a one- or two-word intro, but observe:

Tomorrow Amy will discuss her column. (Who's "Tomorrow Amy"? Use a comma.)

In time travel will be less of a hassle. (Time travel? Again, the comma clarifies.)

- **What goes with what.** In a sentence with more than one introductory clause, skipping the commas helps to hold your points together:

  When he's free of distractions Agassi is the best player in the world, but when he's distracted he's not even among the top 20.

- **Emphasis.** A comma lends a "by the way" quality to an opening clause:

  Of course, you will be allowed to use the restroom.

  Sometimes you want the clause to be more emphatic:

  Of course I need to use the restroom!

THE LOST COMMA

Back when the teaching of English was more regimented, ordinary schoolchildren walked around with terms such as *direct address* in their little heads. Today, the term and the comma that comes with it are nearly lost. *Hi Bill* (or, more likely, *hi bill*) is the standard form for an online greeting. Bill isn't hi, of course, so the comma of direct address makes it *Hi, Bill.* And *Look, Ma, no hands* and *Hey, you* and *Shut up, Stacy.*

THE CARE AND FEEDING OF *And* AND *But*

Many experienced writers and editors don't know the most basic principle guiding whether to use a comma before *and* or *but*. Don't be one of them. Here you go:

Don't use the comma if the subject of the action before the *and* or *but* continues to be the subject afterward. Think of this as the "Amazing Grace" rule:

> *I once was lost but now am found.*

Use the comma if a new subject is introduced or the same subject is restated. If the lyrics were a little different, you'd have:

> *I once was lost, but now I'm found.*

Some secular examples:

> *Garofalo lost weight and found starring roles.*

> *Garofalo disdains Hollywood life, but it pays her rent.*

> *Garofalo is a popular stand-up comic, and she succeeds despite a continuing battle with low self-esteem.*

To put it another way, use a comma if both sides of the sentence could stand as sentences on their own. *Found starring roles* is not a sentence. *It pays her rent* is.

Skip the comma, however, when an imperative statement is followed by a description of something that hinges on the action in the imperative statement:

> *Open this month's Esquire and you'll find Sara Silverman in the "Women We Love" segment.*

Try the seared sea scallops and you'll become a regular at this place.

ADJECTIVE, ADJECTIVE NOUN

Commas with descriptions can be tricky.

I had a glass of sweet orange juice. It's not *sweet, orange juice*: Even though *orange* is, like *sweet*, technically an adjective, in reality *orange juice* acts as a noun, and *sweet* is the only adjective. Some language people would call this a case of adjectives of unequal weight.

The first mystery item was a glass of sweet, green juice. Here, the comma is appropriate. *Sweet* and *green* carry equal weight as adjectives describing *juice*.

I had a glass of sour-cherry juice. Here, the noun is modified by a two-word modifier. The meaning of the sentence isn't that the cherry juice was sour, true as that may be, but that the juice was made of sour cherries. Contrast that with the first orange-juice example, in which it may be true that the juice was made from sweet oranges but the intention was clearly to describe the juice as sweet.

MEET STITCH

I've been called Bill Hyphen Walsh. I've been known to follow the hyphenate-compound-modifiers rule more strictly than most people do. Note that I wrote *orange-juice example* in the previous section; most writers and editors, even the sticklers, probably would have skipped the hyphen. The hyphen is technically correct because the phrase is describing an example about orange juice, not an orange example about juice.

HYPHENATION AND ITS DISCONTENTS

Most writers and editors who give any thought to hyphens at all choose to hyphenate compound modifiers only when skipping the hyphen would produce ambiguity. The classic example is *small-business man* (is the man small, or is the business small?). The clarity-only hyphenators argue that familiar terms such as *orange juice*, *real estate*, *law enforcement* and *high school* are read as single units and therefore require no additional linkage.

Not all of the anti-hyphen forces are so articulate. Most of little Stitch's enemies fall into what I call the "Aw, c'mon, this ain't Wimbleton" category. In my tennis heyday, believe it or not, I was more likely than most players to point out such violations as foot faults and the practice of catching a ball and calling it out rather than actually allowing it to land out. "Aw, c'mon, this ain't Wimbleton," some opponents would retort (such people tend to mispronounce Wimbledon). When you're writing for publication, of course, it pretty much *is* Wimbledon.

Writers and editors often feel strongly about hyphenation when the subject comes up as a matter of policy or in one of their own stories, but I think they overestimate the supposed distraction that strict hyphenation causes for them as readers. I've heard a lot of people praise the Wall Street Journal as a well-written, well-edited newspaper, but I've never heard anyone express annoyance at that newspaper's strict use of the hyphen. The Journal's stylebook has this to say:

The hyphen is helpful to quick understanding even in some frequently used compound modifiers: high-school students, real-estate dealers, stock-market rally, federal-funds rate.

You'll probably end up somewhere in between the Walsh/Journal camp and the hyphenate-only-for-clarity camp, either by your own preference or by the preference of your editor or publisher. But please do read this chapter carefully so you understand the concept.

LONGER-THAN-TWO-WORD MODIFIERS

Even if you do skip hyphens under the "familiar term" principle, the hyphens should be used when that familiar phrase gets absorbed into a larger adjectival phrase. Write *high school education* if you like, but *post-high-school education* works only with both hyphens. Leave out the second one and it looks as if *post-* goes only with *high.* I think of that second hyphen as the Nancy Reagan hyphen, because I once saw somebody write of the former first lady's visit to an *anti-child abuse center.* (It's one thing to be anti-child, but to open *abuse centers?*)

Publications that use the en dash might write *post–high school education.* I don't like that approach, because few readers know that the slightly longer punctuation mark is supposed to jump over words and link them in advance.

LOST SHADES OF MEANING

A casual approach to compound modifiers robs the language of nuance. If *real-estate salesman* were always hyphenated correctly, a salesman who sold something that could truly be called an estate could be called a *real* estate salesman without italics being needed to emphasize the pun. (OK, so *that's* not such a huge loss, but you see my point.)

A DIFFERENT CLARITY ISSUE

British English regularly uses hyphens between adjectives and nouns for the sake of clarity: When the Brits call a bathrobe a *dressing-gown*, they use a hyphen to make it clear that it's a gown *for* dressing, not a gown that *is* dressing. Such hyphens are rare in American English, but they are used in cases of extreme ambiguity. A *giant killer* is a killer who is giant, whereas a *giant-killer* is the killer of a giant.

STITCH IN SUSPENSE

Suspensive hyphenation is the use of hyphens that connect words over a distance. Instead of writing *one-pound and two-pound lobsters*, you can use suspensive hyphenation and make it *one- and two-pound lobsters*. Pay careful attention to the meaning of what you're writing to see whether it calls for suspensive hyphenation or simply one multiple-hyphen modifier:

> *Network-owned and -operated stations* (Some are one, and some are the other.)

> *Network-owned-and-operated stations* (The stations are both owned and operated by the network.)

FLAIR! ELAN! PANACHE!

A Few Potshots About Style-With-a-Capital-S

Try to preserve an author's style if he is an author and has a style.

—Woolcott Gibbs

This chapter could be subtitled "Sober Up, by Dean Martin."

If you've read this far, you know that I'm closer to the "Punch it up a bit" school of writing than I am to "Just the facts, ma'am." I attach a big asterisk to the "Omit needless words" credo from the original "Elements," and I roll my eyes at "Simple, declarative sentences," another mantra that many chant but few follow. I think writing, in most cases, should be writing, not just an owner's-manual-style recitation of what you need to know. I like a little writing with my writing.

But I'm still a tough audience if you're trying to wow me with words. You need to master simple, declarative sentences first. You need to get the facts right before you worry about *writing*-writing. Call me hypocritical for making fun of over-the-top writing if you like, but I'd rather that you reasoned, "Man, if these things annoy *this* guy, they must be *really* bad."

THEM'S WRITIN' WORDS!

I once had an English professor who summed up the difference between *that* and *which* like this: "*Which* sounds more intellectual."

Sounding more intellectual does seem to be the philosophy behind word choice for some writers. Read the "serious" feature stories in a big-time newspaper or its Sunday magazine and note every time you see *some* used instead of *about, said Smith* instead of *Smith said*, and *for his part* and *for her part* and *for their part* whenever an opposing point of view is about to be presented. Get out your yellow highlighter and see if you can build yourself a word-a-day calendar: You'll probably see an *assiduous* here, a *diffident* there, maybe *encomium, jocund, languid, turgid, venial*. And a lot of *indeed*s (I plead guilty on that count). "Intellectual" writing is a form with its own rules, like haiku, except that poetry retains its beauty even for those who know those rules. Once you start looking for the hallmarks of "intellectual" writing, on the other hand, a piece that may have read beautifully starts to look like one big fill-in-the-blanks exercise.

I'm not necessarily against sending readers to the dictionary. In childhood I learned a lot from the Mad magazine

Colors Are Pretty, but How About Just Giving It to Me in Black and White?

We're probably stuck with the Department of Homeland Security's terrorism alert levels (Code Yellow, be worried but not alarmed; Code Orange, be alarmed but not worried; Code Red, run for your lives), but can we stop with the color-coding of more trivial matters? I don't know what the local community center means by "Code Purple" on a snow day, and I doubt that busy families have taken the time to memorize the various systems their various community centers, high schools, middle schools, elementary schools and churches have put into place. Say what you mean, people; you can play your little 007 games on your own time.

of the '70s, which didn't talk down to me. (I knew the word *penumbra* when it came up in a Supreme Court ruling because Mad's "The Shadow Knows" cartoons were listed under "We've Got Your Penumbra Department.") I'm not necessarily against adopting a "literary" tone. But if you find it difficult to imagine the following conversation, you may want to take your intellectualism down a notch:

What Is, Is: Can't Argue With That

Meaningless sentences are meaningless. See? The trouble is, meaninglessness isn't always as obvious as this tautology. The following examples are paraphrased from AM-radio advertising, but you'll find similar nonsense even in more literate media.

> A donation of your car, truck or boat is tax-deductible to the maximum extent of the law.

In other words, you're allowed to deduct it as much as you're allowed to deduct it. Good news: Your toenail clippings are also deductible to the maximum extent of the law.

> The Baldy Center has a 90 percent success rate at growing new hair, guaranteed.

What's that about a guarantee? If you're lying about that success rate, I get my money back? But I didn't give you any money. Are you sure you know what *guarantee* means?

> You can use this scholarship at any participating school in the world.

I have no doubt that this is true. But it raises one major question . . .

"How did things go at work today?"

"I feel languorous. Indeed, I had some nine projects to complete. My boss, whose long, languid face sometimes tightens into a scowl, would hear none of my excuses. For her part, she is niggardly when it comes to blandishment."

TWO VIEWPOINTS ON CLICHES

Never use a metaphor, simile, or other figure of speech which you are used to seeing in print.

—GEORGE ORWELL

Actually we could not avoid the use of cliché even if we wanted to. The very word cliché *is in a sense a cliché—its original meaning is stereotype. And writers on the subject inevitably find themselves using in the discussions words like* coinage, fresh-minted, *and* hackneyed, *all of which are in this same sense clichés.*

—THEODORE M. BERNSTEIN

Bernstein goes on to make good points about when cliches are bad, but I think his semi-defense of cliches is a useful counterpoint to the conventional wisdom.

Steve Coll, managing editor of the Washington Post, has described cliches as first-draft placeholders. You know the point you're trying to make, so you reach for the handiest way of making that point. Later, you go back and substitute a *better* way of saying what you want to say. Coll makes a good point. Bernstein, however, questions whether there always is a better way:

Think of the circumlocution that is avoided by saying that someone has a dog-in-the-manger *attitude. To attempt to write around a cliché will often lead to pompous obscurity. And for a writer to decide to banish all clichés indiscriminately would be to hamstring—yes,* hamstring*—his efforts.*

I have no idea what a dog-in-the-manger attitude might be, which raises another point about cliches: They are perishable.

To improve on that aging example, I offer the phrase *Republicans who rode Bush's coattails.* A story devoted entirely to such politicians could get around the cliche easily enough, but what if this brief reference is the only reference? Might the cliche be better than a circumlocution like *Republicans who were elected partly because of Bush's success?*

More often, I think, writers use cliches for the sake of using cliches. Another example:

Misery loves company. Executives from the battered telecommunications industry, including locally based PluggComm Inc., are gathering in San Francisco this week.

If you're the editor—or the writer, but unsure about what you wrote—what do you do? One option is to stick with the cliche. It's not great, but I've seen worse attempts at catchy openings. Another option is to give the cliche a twist:

Misery loves company, and it appears to be especially fond of PluggComm Inc. The local company, among the most battered in the battered telecommunications sector, sent two top executives to an industry gathering in San Francisco this week.

That's catchier still. If you're going to use a cliche, it's a good idea to let readers know that you know it's a cliche, and one way to do that is by having some fun with it.

An anti-cliche editor might try to make the point in other words:

> *Adversity can bring people together, as illustrated by this week's gathering in San Francisco of executives from battered telecommunications companies, including locally based Plugg-Comm Inc.*

Loses something, doesn't it? When the meaning of a cliche evaporates in the rephrasing, don't be afraid to kill it (or at least save the cliche for the headline, where such idle wordplay is likely to be more prized):

> *Executives from battered telecommunications companies, including locally based PluggComm Inc., are gathering in San Francisco this week.*

Bernstein again:

> *The important thing, however, as must be clear by now, is not to avoid the cliché, but rather to use it only with discrimination and sophistication, and to shun it when it is a substitute for precise thinking.*

CLICHES TODAY

Classics such as *misery loves company*, *selling like hotcakes* and *on thin ice* are the big game of the cliche-hunting world. More modern but right up there are the latest catchphrases from popular culture. The "Saturday Night Live" refrains and

The Spin Wins
Great Moments in Obfuscation

Brevity is nice, but reality is better. The journalistic urge to come up with a short and snappy description for every news item often distorts the truth ("spending cuts" aren't quite the same as "cuts in spending increases," as exasperated conservatives periodically point out), and sometimes it creates instant mythology. My two examples are starting to yellow with age, but they are whoppers.

Bush I's "Slip of the Tongue"

Before the first President Bush became president, he made a campaign stop at an American Legion convention on Sept. 7, 1988, and started talking to the assembled war veterans about how it was the anniversary of the Japanese attack on Pearl Harbor. He realized his error amid murmurs and gestures from the crowd. "Did I say *September 7*? Sorry about that— *December 7, 1941*," Bush said.

Although the news media prominently reported the remarks, many reporters swallowed Bush's impromptu bit of revisionist history, which made the error seem much more minor than it was. The Washington Post said Bush "startled a convention of veterans in Louisville with an embarrassing gaffe, misstating the date of the attack on Pearl Harbor." The New York Times began its story with the words "Vice President Bush made a slip of the tongue today."

But the gaffe was not a misstatement or a slip of the tongue. *September* does rhyme with *December*, and it would be an easy enough mistake to make, but Bush didn't *say* "September"; he *showed up* in September and spoke as though it were December. That's a big difference. If you believe that the news media, and especially the Times and the Post, are biased liberal institutions out to get Republicans, you have to wonder why they let Bush slide on that occasion.

Harding's "Compromise"

In February 1994, after figure skater Nancy Kerrigan was clubbed in the knee by associates of rival skater Tonya Harding, the U.S. Figure Skating Association and the U.S. Olympic Committee started to explore the possibility of excluding Harding from the Olympics. Harding sued the USOC. In what was widely reported as a "compromise," the committee allowed Harding to compete, and in return, Harding dropped her lawsuit.

If the Harding matter was a compromise, we need to rethink our coverage of other events: *An area man agreed to give his wallet to another man yesterday in a compromise in which the second man agreed not to shoot him.*

Harding made a threat, and the USOC backed down. That may not be a crime, but it certainly isn't a compromise. The USOC wanted Harding off the team, and Harding wanted to compete for a medal. If, say, the officials had allowed Harding on the team but only as an alternate, and Harding had agreed, *that* would have been a compromise.

movie dialogue and other lines that are on everyone's lips at any given time are bound to find their way into writing. Use one just before or just *as* the catchphrase is catching on and you might have a winner. After that: *Fuhgeddaboudit.*

Most of your cliche hunting will be much more mundane. Devote yourself to the sport and you'll spend far more time swatting mosquitoes—cliches that are cliches just because the words end up together far more often than chance would dictate. We're talking proximity rather than pith.

The omnipresent identifier is one such class of cliche. *Libyan strongman Moammar Gadhafi* isn't much of a strongman anymore, but we still have *the oil-rich Persian Gulf*; *the tech-heavy, tech-rich* or *tech-laden* (depending on how it's doing) *Nasdaq Stock Market*; and *software giant Microsoft.* Martha Stewart has a host of such descriptions—*domestic diva* (see sidebar in Elephant No. 14) seems to be most popular, but combine *domestic, home, household, home-design* or *home-decorating* with *diva, doyenne, empress, executive, goddess, guru, icon, mogul, queen* or *princess* and you'll see the possibilities.

Zapping these things is sometimes easy. There's nothing wrong with *Libyan leader*, and readers know what Microsoft is. The relative richness in oil or technology stock of the Persian Gulf or the Nasdaq Stock Market can often be made clear in other ways. But what about Martha? Many say we should just let Martha Stewart be Martha Stewart, but who else gets that treatment? Even Muhammad Ali, possibly the most famous human being in recent history, would be *boxing legend* or *former heavyweight champion* on first reference in a story not explicitly sports-related.

Checking the front pages of the Washington Post, the New York Times and the Wall Street Journal on the day I wrote this, I found plenty of word combinations that could be called cliched, but nothing even so interesting as a *domestic diva*. In the Post, people are *on the lam*, fight *an all-out war*, have *their hands forced* and miss their *beloved relatives*. One person *took the plunge*. An epidemic is *sweeping*, arguments are *blunted*, accountability is *clamored for*, gatherings are *tinged with sadness*. Things happened *under cover of darkness*, and a governor *dispatched* police. We have *a wave of violence* and *a grave crisis*.

In the Times, something generates *serious buzz*. There's an *everything from* that never gets around to a *to*. Somebody is *riding high*, but there's a *rude awakening* as well as *smug complacency*. And a *train wreck* that doesn't involve trains. Demons are *unleashed*, and there's a *diplomatic swing*.

The Journal features *loose lips* and a *clash of titans*. Somebody *strays from the script*. It's *all quiet* on one front, but we get a *view from the ground*.

You know what? Aside from the *everything from* line, I'm not sure I would have changed any of those. I try to avoid cliches, but I agree with Bernstein that it's pointless to try to eliminate them entirely. And I suspect that the writers and editors most hostile to colorful language when it's stale would also be the most hostile to colorful language when it's fresh. Try getting a newly coined figure of speech past a cliche-hating editor.

Openings You've Seen Before, and Other Cliched Approaches

Sometimes a cliche is more than just a phrase—it's an approach. Such shopworn approaches often show up in lead paragraphs ("ledes" in newspaper jargon). This is where writers try hardest to show off, so it's also where they're most likely to stumble. Plenty of writers and editors could put this book down and list the tired, illogical and otherwise annoying opening gambits that keep getting filed by inexperienced writers who don't know any better as well as experienced ones who should know better. My list:

THE DICTIONARY DEFINITION

Webster's Dictionary defines "hero" as "one that shows great courage." Jim Wrubel, who saved a kitten from a tree yesterday, undoubtedly fits that definition.

In addition to being a cliched device, dictionary ledes tend to be overwrought and tend to invent a nonexistent "Webster's Dictionary" (see "Webster" in the Curmudgeon's Stylebook chapter).

Welcome to the World Of

Dirty plates piled as high as the eye can see. Steam above and fetid water below, for eight, nine, 10 hours at a time. Indecent proposals from male co-workers. Minimum wage and no tips. Welcome to the world of dishwasher Jillian Barnes.

Not Alone

Michelle Goins started seeing unfamiliar charges on her Visa card last summer. She started calling around and soon learned she had been a victim of identity theft. Goins is not alone.

THE TERM PAPER

Throughout history, man has struggled with the problem of finding enough food to eat. The latest figures from the Census Bureau show that this struggle continues, especially in the nation's big cities.

THE WASTED LINE

Here we go again.

I couldn't agree more. Now get to the point. This kind of opening is especially popular among columnists.

It happens every time.

Color me [blank].

Psst.

NO, IT'S NOT

When Charles Dickens wrote, "It was the best of times, it was the worst of times," he was undoubtedly thinking of the Cleveland suburb of Shaker Heights.

No, he wasn't.

Area schools will be back in session Monday, disappointing thousands of children who would rather stay home and watch John Wayne movies.

No, they wouldn't. (How old are you, anyway?)

The City Council passed a parking-meter law that is bound to create more problems than it solves. It's called parkus interruptus.

No, it's not. This is how a lot of columnists think terms are coined. If you're coining a term, make it clear that you're doing so. *Call it parkus interruptus* would do the trick, or simply drop the term into a sentence. Something isn't "called" something until a significant number of people have done the calling.

THE LITERARY ALLUSION

The Class 2 state girls' basketball tournament has been a tale of two cities.

THE LITERARY ILLUSION

Newspaper feature sections, women's magazines and airline magazines are excellent sources of breathless, unnecessarily dramatic writing. When you write something that sounds as though it could be read in a faux-solemn tone in the first minute of a low-budget cable-TV documentary, it's time to start over.

Pity the poor foot. Hauling each and every pound of you around for 10, 12, maybe 14 hours a day, all the while cooped up in a sweaty sarcophagus. It's no wonder experts say the feet are the most overworked part of the body.

Any sentence or lede beginning with "Pity the poor" is going to be trouble, but feet, for some reason, are a classic source of bright-and-breezy-magaziney writing. Perhaps it's because they loom so large in women's magazines. And then there's the predictability of such stories. Buy a bunch of those magazines as warm weather approaches and see how many lecture you on how it's time to get ready to "expose those toes" by cutting your nails "straight across" after you wash your feet with "a mild soap" and "blot, don't rub" them dry with a fluffy towel.

The theme of change, usually contrived, is big in this kind of writing:

> *Spas, once the province of pampered heiresses and Hollywood starlets, aren't just for the rich anymore.*

Another example:

> *From its position as the humble mainstay on the Irish dinner table, the potato has risen to star status.*

Um, OK.

THE RODNEY DANGERFIELD OF [BLANK]

Yeah, we get it: [Blank] don't get no respect. You might think using Rodney Dangerfield as a metaphor is a fad whose time passed in the 1980s, but it lives on. A recent check of the LexisNexis database found mentions of Rodney in North American publications—though not always in ledes—running at about one per day.

All in a one-month period: Italy is the Rodney Dangerfield of Europe. "The lowly candle" is the Rodney Dangerfield of home lighting. Coots are the Rodney Dangerfield of the bird world. Film composers are like Rodney Dangerfield. Lt. Gov. John Cherry is the Rodney Dangerfield of Michigan politics (*and* the state's higher-education community is the Rodney Dangerfield of Michigan government). Canadian Western Bank "has long suffered from Rodney Dangerfield syndrome" (*and* westerners are the Rodney Dangerfield of Canada). District 11 is the Rodney Dangerfield of Denver (and Denver is the Rodney Dangerfield of fine dining). Reality TV is the Rodney Dangerfield of broadcasting. Carnations are the Rodney Dangerfield of the flower world. "Utilitarian folding tables and chairs" are like Rodney Dangerfield because they "don't tend to show up in glossy magazine spreads." One college-hockey goalie *isn't* about to become the Rodney Dangerfield of that sport's championships. One columnist is the Rodney Dangerfield of e-commerce. California's Central Valley is the Rodney Dangerfield of agriculture. Rochester, N.Y., is the Rodney Dangerfield of Thruway Travel. The IUD is the Rodney Dangerfield of birth control. Potatoes "could be" the Rodney Dangerfield of side dishes. Fox "risks being seen as" the Rodney Dangerfield of journalism. "Until recently," the Chisholm Trail was the Rodney Dangerfield of Texas tourism. Rodney Dangerfield's lament "could also apply to the Spanish bayonet plant." New Jersey "might as well be" the Rodney Dangerfield of states. In the United States, the French are feeling like Rodney Dangerfield. Buddy Gil is the Rodney Dangerfield of horse racing. Cabernet franc has been the Rodney Dangerfield of red-wine grapes.

And my favorite: "If the tuba were a stand-up comic, the instrument undoubtedly would be Rodney Dangerfield." (*Undoubtedly*, like *literally*, is a bold bluff of an intensifier, usually used to insist on the truth of something very much not true.)

Madam Chairman and That Friggin' Masseuse
Taking Linguistic Evolution Like a "-man"

Don't call a woman a man. But, then again, don't go out of your way to point out that she's a woman.

That's the best I can do in trying to come up with a guideline for avoiding a perception of sexism in language, a goal that resists guidelines. Gender-specific terms insist on being evaluated individually. The conclusions that you or I come up with will seem inconsistent, but that shouldn't be surprising. English can be wacky, the things people do and don't take offense at can be wacky, and the hard-line positions of both traditionalists and reformers can be wacky.

-Man, Oh, *-Man*

Terms ending in *-man* were once thought to be gender-neutral. In *chairman* and *spokesman*, *man* meant "man" not in the sense of "You're a woman, I'm a man—let's make beautiful music together," but in the sense of "Throughout history, man has . . ." You can't really fault people for thinking *man* means "man," though, and as *-men* increasingly became women, the evolution of such terms was inevitable.

Businessman is clearly inappropriate as a term for a woman, and it probably always was. Even the pronunciation makes that clear: Compare the "man" of *businessman* with the "mun" of *chairman* and *spokesman*. There's nothing wrong with *businesswoman* if you're writing about one, but the neutral *business owner* and *executive* make *businessman* easy to avoid. And, if you really need such a word, *businessperson* and *businesspeople* are less goofy-looking than some of the other -*person* forms.

Chairman survives, though more often as a job title than as a generic description. Many corporate boards and organizations have a position called *chairman*, and it's called that whether a man or a woman holds the post. If a woman is running something less formal, though, it makes more sense to use *chairwoman*. This could change over the years, but at the moment the term has retained enough gender-neutral credibility that the plural *chairmen* works even for positions whose female occupants would be called chairwomen. *Chairperson* is unnecessary. Avoid the "I'd rather be a piece of furniture than a man!" connotation of *chair* unless it's a formal title (as it is, interestingly, at the Equal Employment Opportunity Commission).

Spokesman is somewhere in between. Seldom is it a job title (the real titles tend to be "executive vice president for communications," "media liaison" and other euphemistic bombast), so *spokeswoman* should be used for women. To me, calling a specific woman a spokesman is calling her a man. The generic sense, however, has survived to some extent: I think it's fine to use *spokesman* as a generic term and *spokesmen* as a mixed-company plural. There is no need to resort to *spokesperson* or *spokespersons* or *spokespeople*.

The -ess Mess

The other category of troublesome gender-specific terms is the female suffix. *Aviatrix*, *poetess* and even *comedienne* look ridiculous today, but parallel examples survive.

Waitress is under siege by the proponents of *waitron* and *waitstaff*, but for now it's a respectable word. *Waitron* and the like are silly because, among other things, there's nothing inherently male in the term *waiter*. *Server* works if you need a generic term.

Actress, too, survives, even though there's nothing inherently male in *actor* either. Still, maybe it's just me, but when female performers refer to themselves as "actors" it just sounds wrong, and a little pretentious. Most of the award shows still use *actress*, and I think the separate terms may survive indefinitely because actors and actresses, like mothers and fathers, are not interchangeable. A male waiter could be replaced by a female waiter (that doesn't sound so bad, does it?) and a comedian is a comedian, but actors and actresses play different roles, so to speak.

Hostess still looks fine for a woman throwing a party, but Oprah is a talk-show *host*.

Masseuse and *chanteuse* survive because they come from French, a language in which all nouns have gender. Because English speakers hear *masseuse* far more often than *masseur*, the use of the feminine term for male massage therapists is a common error. (Fans of "reality" television may remember "Temptation Island" contestant Andy cursing one rival for his woman's affection as "that friggin' masseuse.") *Massage therapist*, of course, avoids the gender issue. It also avoids the sex issue—*masseuse*, like *massage parlor*, can have an illicit connotation.

His-Tory

And then there's the personal pronoun. If I say *each authority has his opinion*, am I excluding Barbara Wallraff and Patricia O'Conner and Constance Hale? Of course not, but it does sort of sound that way. The use of male pronouns as the gender-neutral default is a dying tradition, but that problem is easier said than solved. *Each authority has his or her opinion* is unnatural and unwieldy. *Each authority has his/her opinion* is more multiple-choice exam than writing. *Each authority has her opinion* has the same problem as the traditional usage and sounds patronizing to boot. *Each authority has their opinion*, which applies a plural pronoun to a singular antecedent, will have many people reaching for the dunce cap, but it's clearly the best of the imperfect solutions. I think the *them/they/their/theirs* solution will eventually become standard. Because English has no official panel to set the rules, however, right-thinking pioneers will have to endure the scorn of the traditionalists for now.

There's always the write-around-it solution: *All authorities have their own opinions. Each authority has an opinion.*

WRITERS, TYPISTS, THIEVES AND LIARS

Plagiarism and Its Kin

That's not writing, that's typing.

—Truman Capote, on the work of Jack Kerouac

A re you a writer or a typist?

I don't mean that in the Capote-on-Kerouac sense. I mean that in the sense of "I'm typing in some press releases," a sentence that should be uttered only by someone who *writes* such releases. (They're actually *news* releases now that the press isn't the only news medium, but typists who think they're writers aren't likely to grasp such distinctions.)

STEALING STUFF

"Typing in" something written by someone else rather than using it as a starting point for your own writing doesn't automatically make you a Jayson Blair, but it puts you in the same phylum, in my taxonomy. There's theft of the kind that can get you in legal trouble, such as copying published material and claiming it as your own, and then there's theft that is officially sanctioned, but they're both theft. The news-release people *want* you to publish their news releases precisely the way they wrote them. That's free advertising! The Associated Press would prefer to be credited, but if you're working for a news organization that subscribes to its wire service, you have bought the rights to that writing, and you can do with it as you wish. (This is a slightly different issue, but if you're an editor who writes photo captions and you generally just "type in" whatever the photographer wrote—or if you even refer to what the photographer wrote as "a caption" rather than "caption information"—you're just stupid.)

I'm not a lawyer. The copyright issue makes little difference to me. The issue is whether you have the right to call yourself a writer. If you publish a sentence any more complex than *The meeting will be held Thursday at 3 p.m.* under your name or your publication's banner, the wording of that sentence had better be original to you or your publication.

"But, Bill," you say, "with all the wars and the starvation and the pain and suffering in the world, does it really matter whether the wording of two sentences about Sunday's potluck supper in the Podunk Town Crier differs from the wording in the church bulletin?"

Yes.

Reporting and research are usually anything but original, at the Town Crier or the Washington Post. Even the best reporters seldom actually discover facts on their own; they get facts by digging through documents written by others, or by befriending, cajoling, tricking or even intimidating people who then pass facts along. That's reporting. Writing is another matter. It is a matter of honor that writers do their own writing. If a writer places a byline on that writing, it's more than a matter of honor; it's a matter of honesty.

It's also a matter of accuracy. Do you know that the information in the news release is correct? When I work with typists who consider themselves reporters, I have to deal with calendar listings in which the same hotel appears two or three times with two or three different names and two or three different addresses, depending on what version of the name or address the news release contained. Write! Report! Verify!

If you're such a piss-poor writer that you can't improve on, or at least reword, a news release, you might want to consider another career.

I'll say it again: I believe Kinko's is hiring.

MAKING UP STUFF

Not-quite-memoir memoirs are blurring the line between fiction and nonfiction, but you know the drill: Journalists aren't supposed to make things up. Nonfiction with a little fiction thrown in should include a note making that clear.

You're probably pretty sure you're not a big, fat liar, so the following rant may be news to you:

Changing a quotation to correct someone's grammar may not make you a Stephen Glass, but, again—same phylum.

If you're interviewing someone who says, "I ain't got no problem with them there neighbors," you may write:

"I ain't got no problem with them there neighbors," he said.

And you may write:

He said he has "no problem" with his neighbors.

And I wouldn't advise it, for aesthetic reasons, but you'd be on solid ethical ground to write:

"I . . . got no problem with . . . [the] neighbors," he said.

But you may *not* write:

"I have no problem with the neighbors," he said.

That would be lying. He did *not* say that.

WRITING AND
REWRITING

*A Writer-Turned-Editor Writes About
Editing and Being Edited*

Some editors are failed writers, but so are most writers.

—T.S. ELIOT

Editing should be invisible.

Most readers—if they even know editors exist—have no idea just how different what appears under a writer's byline can be from what the writer actually wrote. And that's a good thing. An article should speak with a single voice. If I pick up Martha Stewart Living magazine to read about Martha's philosophy on potpourri, I don't want to be tapped on the shoulder and interrupted in the middle of the essay.

*Joanne here, assistant associate managing editor/research and copy. I think what Martha meant to say was . . . (*Tell you what, Joanne: You and Martha straighten things out and get back to me.)

That may sound like an extreme example, but something similar happened to me. In an article for a newsletter on writing and editing, I mentioned, with a little hyperbole, having worked for an editor who was the kind of guy who would insist *television* wasn't a word because it wasn't in his aging copy of the Oxford English Dictionary. A sharp-eyed editor noted that *television* appeared in the OED long before television as we know it was invented. Good catch, but then things went way wrong. What you do at that point if you're the sharp-eyed editor is ask the writer for a similar example that makes the same point but isn't in a 20- or 30-year-old copy of the OED. *Microwave* might have worked, or maybe *Internet*. Instead, he added a footnote pointing out that *television*, albeit with a different meaning, did indeed appear in the OED a long time ago.

As an editor, you do sometimes feel as if you weren't invited to the party. But you should have already known that when you took the job, and editing is by definition a behind-the-scenes job. Sometimes it's a creative, prestigious behind-the-scenes job, and sometimes it's a lowly, grunt-work behind-the-scenes job, but either way you have to get out of the shot and let the actors be the center of attention. Your job is to make the writer look good, not to point out to the readers that the writer isn't exactly an expert on the subject matter or the stylebook or the dictionary. If you write headlines or captions that accompany articles, your job is to make those headlines or captions sound as though the writers wrote them—even if the writer is simply a reader whose letter you are publishing (headlines on letters to the editor should never include anything like *Reader Says*).

Another personal anecdote with a moral:

When I was a reporting intern and didn't know any better, I led a story with a "phoenix rising from the ashes" line— a cliche in any city, but an especially tired one in Phoenix. One of my editors killed the first paragraph, quite correctly— and then he simply started the story with the second paragraph. The cut-from-the-top approach is a common solution for too-cute openings and a handy solution on deadline, but I think of it as a parlor trick rather than good editing. When there's time, a good editor who doesn't like a writer's opening lines asks the writer for a Plan B or a Plan C. That might be a futile tactic if the writer is the kind of doofus who would write about a phoenix rising from the ashes, but there's a good chance that the writer's second-favorite opening might be better than a line that wasn't designed to be an opening. Editing isn't a game in which you try to make a story publishable in as few moves as possible. Often it's better to rewrite a sentence entirely than to try to repair a problem by rearranging the words.

In the Curmudgeon's Stylebook chapter of this book I take issue with *homicide bombing*, a term offered by those offended by the focus on the killer inherent in *suicide bombing*. The edit that produced the substitute term wasn't made by an editor, of course, but it's a perfect example of the as-few-moves-as-possible school of bad editing: "Hey, look: By changing just one syllable . . ."

From *From* to *To*
Everything's Ranging

A Scripps Howard story on actor John Leguizamo mentions that he "has starred in films and TV projects ranging from 'Moulin Rouge' to 'Arabian Nights.'" Let's see, how does that continuum go again? Oh, yes, there's "Moulin Rouge," then "The Incredible Mr. Limpet," "Davey and Goliath," "Gonorrhea and You: A Cautionary Tale," and then finally "Arabian Nights."

What we have here is a false range. Plug "ranging" or "everything" into a search engine and you'll find plenty of examples (because some stupid interfaces won't let you do a true full-text search for "ranging *from*" or "everything *from*," though, it might take a little sifting).

Ranges can be valid, of course. *From New York to Los Angeles* traces a geographic path; there are places in between. *All Chevrolets, from the entry-level Cavalier to the muscular Corvette* paints a clear picture. *From Allison to Zelda* requires a little artistic license, but at least it has an alphabetical reference point. When you're told, however, that a store sells merchandise ranging from diapers to snow tires, there is no such "range." If the variety of merchandise is worth mentioning, there are other ways to mention it.

The *everything from* phrase has the added problem of not excluding *anything*. I'm not sure where the soundtrack from

"Don't Tell Mom the Babysitter's Dead" fits in the panoply of "everything from be-bop to unsigned bands" (the Wall Street Journal's description of what's available on satellite radio), but you can't tell me it's not in there somewhere. And when my paper, the Washington Post, says "everything from fantasy to animation to suspense dramas" was popular at the movies in 2001, that necessarily includes straight-to-video Frank Stallone crap, NC-17 films involving barnyard animals, and propaganda documentaries denying the Holocaust. Remember: It says "everything"!

Even if you pooh-pooh my criticism of this device as overly literal, you must admit that *from . . . to*, with or without *everything* or *ranging*, is a tired technique. Variety is interesting, but would you really write "Variety is the spice of life!" with a straight face once in an article, let alone more than once?

Like all crutches, though, *from . . . to* is easy to lean on. I must admit I heard complaints about false ranges for several years before they resonated with me. So I sit humbly prepared to have my own writing combed for everything ranging from *everything* to *ranging*.

Snarky Specificity

Remember Zoe, the girl you puked on at the Pink Flamingo Motor Lodge on spring break? Me neither.

There are cliched expressions, and there are cliched writing techniques. (Some would include in the latter category the "There are *x*, and there are *y*" technique. Or the "Some would include" technique. Or the repetition of *or*. Or the parenthetical aside. Somebody slap me.)

While it's a noble goal to rid writing of cliches, I'm not sure it's possible to be completely successful. Once you broaden the definition of *cliche* to include writing techniques (as you should), even conventional sentence structure starts to look like a cliche. It's been done before, right?

I think it's important, then, to sharpen your cliche-hunting focus and target phrases and techniques not just because they've been done before (very little has never been done before), but because they're especially tired or annoying. This isn't, to use a cliche, an exact science. I might be just fine with a certain technique in one piece of writing but be determined to zap it in another piece of writing.

One currently popular device that I think deserves a wary eye is what I have dubbed the smirkingly specific example. You've encountered this device, I'm sure—if not in actual writing, then in television and radio commercials. Its users

(and I've been among them) consider it a tool of moderniza-
tion. At one time it was. Now, at least to me, it increasingly
comes across as self-consciously cute and annoying. (And
when *I* think something is self-consciously cute, well . . .)

Here's a decidedly non-modern sentence:

Visitors sometimes tell boring stories.

Here's how the same idea looks after it's been through the
Smirkingly Specific Modernizator®:

*Tired of listening to Uncle Harry go on and on about his
nose-hair collection?*

You get the idea. This device isn't always so slapstick. Sometimes it's just a little more cutely specific than it should be.
The genesis of this rant, in fact, was a very mild example I
encountered at work—something about "distance learning"
being used by adults, not just eighth-graders. Of course, the
writer didn't really mean to exclude sixth- and ninth- and
other-graders; she was just trying to be a little cute. At one
time I would have thought she had succeeded. Now I'm just
a little tired of reading such things.

My brother Terence at the East Valley Tribune in Mesa,
Ariz., points to the conspicuous use of *that* and *those* as
another hallmark of this device. Instead of instructing readers that a tidy car is a good thing, writers of the new school
might harangue people whose cars they have never seen
about "that McDonald's bag" or "those soda cans" cluttering
their backseats. Terence notes that this kind of specificity
renders writing inaccurate as well as silly: Most readers have
neither an uncle named Harry nor a McDonald's-wrapper-
littered car.

Literal and Conservative
George Washington Wasn't *Really* Our Father

When Martha Stewart's name was mentioned in an insider-trading scandal and Stewart moved to the business section from what used to be called the "women's pages," writers got creative in describing to readers who might not be familiar with Stewart what exactly it is she does for a living. *Domestic diva* was one popular description.

The we-take-everything-literally brigade doesn't take anything lightly, and this was no exception. Stewart, it turns out, is not "(n.) a leading woman singer, esp. in grand opera."

Where do I begin to argue with that logic?

In other news, Aretha Franklin is neither the queen of soul nor any other form of royalty. Babe Ruth, likewise, may have had plenty of swat, but he was no sultan—that is, "(n.) a Muslim ruler." Ted Williams, a splendid splinter? Uh-uh. He was no more made of wood than Mike Tyson was made of iron.

Good news for diabetics: The various Sugar Rays are safe. One of them, however, is telling us that Marvin Hagler wasn't all that marvelous.

The Editor's Curse
While I part ways with many of my copy-editing colleagues in saying there's nothing wrong with calling Martha Stewart a

domestic diva (though the appellation got old pretty fast), I can relate to the literalist instinct. As a copy editor you *must* read things literally to make sure they make sense. Throughout both of my books I urge readers not to memorize the names of parts of speech but to take a close look at the sentence in question and ask whether it literally means what the writer intended it to mean. Here are a couple of cases where literalism served me well, both taken from personal-finance columns:

> *Jim Kelsoe's $116 million Morgan Keegan High Income Fund had the biggest gain among high-yield bond funds for the second year in a row in 2001 because the 38-year-old manager says he avoided corporate debt.*

The fund did well because of what the manager *said*? Here, a literal reading reveals faulty sentence construction. The edited version:

> *Jim Kelsoe's $116 million Morgan Keegan High Income Fund had the biggest gain among high-yield bond funds for the second year in a row in 2001, and the 38-year-old manager credits his avoidance of corporate debt.*

In another case, a columnist wrote about how "plastic has become uncool" at Citibank. She described a new card for online purchases that "acts like a credit card, but exists only in Citi's computer."

I had one of those cards, and although it wasn't meant to be carried around and used at stores, it was an actual physical card that Citibank mailed to me, and it was made of plastic. So I took out the "uncool" reference and simply said that the card is solely for Web transactions.

Plastic has come to be synonymous with *credit card*, but it will always be synonymous with *plastic*. In the column in question, slang collided with reality. If you were writing about a man so poor he subsists on two-day-old pumpernickel from a bakery trash bin, it would be especially silly to use the slang term *bread* to mean money. Yes, the guy has no money, but he does have bread. And I had plastic.

Excessive Explanation

A close relative to extreme literalism is the habit of explaining things way too much. When I see writers and editors do this, I think of Walter Mondale. It was bad enough when Mondale chose "Where's the beef?" as his rallying cry during the 1984 Democratic primaries, but did he have to preface that with something like "As the well-known hamburger advertisement goes . . ."? We reveal our inner Mondale when we insist on annotating quotes. If you must use the quote "At least there ain't no hanky-panky like with Clinton and Lewinsky," please resist the temptation to make it "At least there [isn't any] hanky-panky [as] with [then-President Bill] Clinton and [former intern Monica] Lewinsky." Let quotes be quotes. If the quote needs annotation, it isn't worth using.

One Meaning Per Word

Another related issue is the misguided notion that certain words have only one meaning, despite ample evidence of the multiple meanings of both those disputed words and countless words whose multiple meanings are not in dispute. In the AP Stylebook you will find examples of the one-meaning-per-word fetish in the entries for *hike* and *suit*. To use *hike* to mean "increase" isn't elegant, but it's undeniably valid. *Lawsuit* should be spelled out on first reference if possible, but *suit* can certainly mean the same thing.

Judgment Calls

Many of the entries in this book are about walking the fine line between precise writing and dorky literalism. As I'm defending *domestic diva*, am I clinging to the one-meaning-per-word myth when I insist that *such as* is different from *like*? Are *Uncle Harry's nose-hair collection* and *films and TV projects ranging from "Moulin Rouge" to "Arabian Nights"* examples of time-honored rhetorical figures? These are close calls. In each case I have tried to make an argument that works even if you do think I'm being too literal in my primary objection to such usages.

THE CURMUDGEON'S
STYLEBOOK
(CONTINUED)

The last chapter of "Lapsing Into a Comma" was the Curmudgeon's Stylebook, an opinionated, alphabetical guide to interesting but often obscure questions of usage and miscellaneous facts interspersed with even more opinionated articles. Here, that stylebook continues.

ABOUT, AT ABOUT The traditional guideline is to omit the *at*: *We arrived about 7:30.*

It's tempting to question that, as I did for a long time, because if you subtract the qualifier, you get *We arrived 7:30,* which is clearly incorrect except in airline jargon.

But I've come around to the traditional viewpoint. Something can happen *at* 7:30, but there is no time called *about* *7:30*, so something cannot happen *at* that time. The word *about*, then, contains the idea of "at," the same way *around* or *in the neighborhood of* does. You'd say someone lives *in Cleveland* or *around Cleveland*, not *in around Cleveland*.

ACTUALLY *Actually* is the new *like*.

> **SO, LIKE, FIVE MINUTES AGO:** *"Caitlin, like, got her, like, tongue pierced."*
>
> **ACTUALLY, NOW:** *"Actually, Caitlin actually got her tongue pierced."*

What this (actually) means for (actual) writing is that what used to be an innocuous, if sometimes superfluous, intensifier will now appear to some readers as a sign of questionable intelligence.

ADMINISTRATION Watch out for *adminstration*, a common typographical error.

ADVANCE, ADVANCED *Advanced* means "at a higher level." Do not use it to mean "in advance": It's *advance tickets* and *advance-purchase requirements*.

AFGHAN, AFGHANI I covered this in "Lapsing Into a Comma," but with the increase in news about Afghanistan it bears repeating: Although the people of Pakistan are *Pakistanis*, the people of Afghanistan are *Afghans*. The word *afghani* refers solely to the country's main unit of currency. To call an Afghan an afghani is like calling an American a dollar.

AIRPLANES, FLYING THEM THROUGH THINGS It used to be cute, if cliched, to write about loopholes "big enough to fly a plane through." It seems obvious to me that the phrase is no longer cute, but I found at least one writer trying to use it a few months after Sept. 11, 2001.

AND I If you think "grammar" when you hear "style," this could be the biggest elephant of all. A lot of people, misapplying a childhood correction, think the words *and me* automatically constitute bad grammar, that the expression must always be *and I*. Or maybe you tried to learn the rule behind such things but gave up amid a fusillade of talk about nominative this and objective that. Forget the teacher-speak, and look at it this way: Simply drop the other person from your sentence, and see whether *I* or *me* makes sense:

> *a. Thelma and I are throwing a dinner party.*
> *b. Thelma and me are throwing a dinner party.*

Get rid of Thelma and you have:

> *a. I [am] throwing a dinner party.*
> *b. Me [am] throwing a dinner party.*

It is *I*. The correct answer is (a).

> *a. Join Thelma and I for a dinner party.*
> *b. Join Thelma and me for a dinner party.*

Get rid of Thelma and you have:

> *a. Join I for a dinner party.*
> *b. Join me for a dinner party.*

It is *me*. The correct answer is (b).

ANNUAL *Annual* isn't a horribly pretentious word, but often it's less stilted to simply say "a year":

ACCEPTABLE: *The company announced that it will lay off 5,000 employees as part of an effort to cut $2.5 billion in annual spending.*

BETTER: *The company announced that it will lay off 5,000 employees as part of an effort to cut spending by $2.5 billion a year.*

ANTENNAS, ANTENNAE Insects have *antennae*. Cars and cellphones and other things with more than one antenna have *antennas*.

ANYWHERE FROM ... As much as I like conversational writing, there are conventions of conversation that just don't belong in print. For instance:

The fee is anywhere from 99 cents to $1.50.

Anywhere, eh? So sometimes it's 99 cents, sometimes it's $1, sometimes it's $1.01, sometimes it's $1.02, sometimes it's $1.03, sometimes it's $1.04, sometimes it's $1.05, sometimes it's $1.06, sometimes it's $1.07, sometimes it's $1.08, sometimes it's $1.09, sometimes it's $1.10, sometimes it's $1.11, sometimes it's $1.12, sometimes it's $1.13, sometimes it's $1.14, sometimes it's $1.15, sometimes it's $1.16, sometimes it's $1.17, sometimes it's $1.18, sometimes it's $1.19, sometimes it's $1.20, sometimes it's $1.21, sometimes it's $1.22, sometimes it's $1.23, sometimes it's $1.24, sometimes it's $1.25, sometimes it's $1.26, sometimes it's $1.27, sometimes it's $1.28, sometimes it's $1.29, sometimes it's $1.30, sometimes it's $1.31, sometimes it's $1.32, sometimes it's $1.33, sometimes it's $1.34, sometimes it's $1.35, sometimes it's $1.36, sometimes it's $1.37, sometimes it's $1.38, sometimes it's $1.39, sometimes it's $1.40, sometimes it's $1.41, sometimes it's $1.42, sometimes it's $1.43, sometimes it's $1.44, sometimes it's $1.45, sometimes it's $1.46, sometimes it's $1.47, sometimes it's $1.48, sometimes it's $1.49 and sometimes it's $1.50.

I doubt it.

APPROXIMATELY *About* is shorter, less pretentious and usually better, but *approximately* has its place. After a pronoun or an article, *about* just doesn't work:

> *The company plans to lay off about half of its approximately 10,000 employees.* (*Its about 10,000 employees?* I don't think so.)

> *Police handcuffed two of the approximately 150 protesters.* (*The about?* No.)

AS [SOMEBODY] SAYS This isn't just another way to introduce a quote. It makes sense only if the speaker makes a point that the writer agrees with. If you're writing about death-row inmate Darrell Wayne Grimm and Grimm says a truism, something that you, the writer, might have said yourself, fine:

> *As Grimm says, "tomorrow is another day."*

But you're a bad, bad person in addition to being a bad, bad writer if you write:

> *As Grimm says, "all women are whores who deserve to be decapitated."*

Note the lowercase letter at the beginning of the partial quote. That's not just an arbitrary style mandate; it's central to the point I just made. Start with *Grimm says* or *Grimm said* and you're introducing Grimm's quote. Start with *As Grimm says* and you're making the point yourself but using Grimm's words. Those words are part of the sentence as a whole, not a detached quote within the sentence, and thus they make up a partial quote. Partial quotes don't begin with capital letters.

AS SOON AS　Some curmudgeons blanch at any appearance of *as soon as*, but this phrase has its place. The certainty that an important event will happen soon would be bigger news, but the *possibility* of that immediacy is news as well. Things go way wrong, however, when writers mix possibility with certainty. Read enough newspapers and you'll find plenty of examples like this:

> *The Securities and Exchange Commission will announce as early as tomorrow an investigation of accounting practices at EWebDotNet.com.*

The obvious fix is to change *will* to *could* or *may*. If the writer is sure that the event will happen but unsure of when, it can be handled this way:

> *The Securities and Exchange Commission will announce, possibly as early as tomorrow, an investigation of accounting practices at EWebDotNet.com.*

Attribution of some sort would solve another problem with such a flat-out prediction. See WILL for a caution about forecasting the future.

AT THE END OF THE DAY The cliche gods have apparently decreed that this expression replaces "when all is said and done." Days do end, so the phrase can't really be banned, but be aware that it is a cliche.

BLUE BLOOD, BLUEBLOOD Obviously it's two words in *He has blue blood*, but what about the noun for those who have blue blood? The major dictionaries prefer *blue blood*, but this flies in the face of the way such nouns are built (*greenback, graybeard, redcoat, whitehead*). In a rare call for civil disobedience and a rare vote for onewordization, I say that the rich people in question are *bluebloods*. *Blue blood* is blood that is blue. See ROUND TABLE, ROUNDTABLE and YELLOW JACKET, YELLOWJACKET.

BLUE JEANS, BLUEJEANS Are you more interested in looks or in philosophical consistency? To me, *blue jeans* looks correct. But a strong argument can be made for *bluejeans*, which emphasizes the fundamental difference between that term and *green jeans* or *black jeans*, in which the color is an incidental detail rather than an integral part of the pants' identity. Webster's New World, the dictionary used by most newspapers, goes with *bluejeans*. Merriam-Webster and American Heritage prefer *blue jeans*.

(BOB'S) BIG BOY The iconic restaurant chain is Big Boy, which is also the name of its roly-poly mascot. The mascot isn't named Bob, and only some of the restaurants are called Bob's Big Boy. In Detroit, for example, it's Elias Brothers' Big Boy. In Cincinnati it's Frisch's Big Boy.

B2B Business-to-business transactions are *business-to-business transactions*. If someone is quoted talking about B-to-B, it's *B-to-B*. Why not use *B2B*? Because you're not Prince. Why don't we hear about B-to-B commerce as much as we used to? Because it's not 1999. (Why don't we hear about Prince as much as we used to? Same reason.)

CAR-RENTAL COMPANIES A subtle distinction, perhaps, but they aren't *rental-car companies*. You wouldn't call a place that rents bicycles a "rental-bike place," but because the phrase *rental car* (with an assist, perhaps, from the *rent a car* that appears in car-rental companies' names) has become so familiar, people often say "rental-car companies" when they're talking about car-rental companies. See also HARD-HIT.

CELLPHONE The transition from *cell phone* has been blessed by the fourth edition of Webster's New World College Dictionary, and I'll grudgingly go along, if only because the newfangled formation eliminates the widespread omission of the hyphen that would be necessary in *cell-phone users*, *cell-phone companies* and other adjectival usages. The British *mobile phone* is more logical, but that would raise the hyphen issue again.

CITIES, STATES, COUNTRIES, ETC. *The company has offices in London and France.* If you don't know where in France, sacrifice specificity for consistency and write *England and France* so you don't give the impression that you think London is a country or France is a city.

COFFEE SHOP Use the term advisedly. Starbucks outlets are shops that sell coffee, but are they really coffee shops? I think of a coffee shop as a Denny's-style establishment, a casual restaurant that serves a diverse menu including breakfast all day. Often it's part of a hotel or other larger establishment. Starbucks and its competitors are better referred to as *coffee bars*.

CONTINUED In courtroom jargon, *continued* means "postponed." In descriptions of courtroom activity intended for normal people, use *postponed*.

COPY EDITORS, COPYEDITORS AND IRONY Copy editors (two words, please) are supposed to promote readability and eschew jargon. They're also supposed to make sure *ironic* isn't used to mean "coincidental," but I find it darn close to truly ironic that some copy editors choose to inflict the unreadable and jargony *copyeditor* and *copyediting* on readers. (In general, copy editors in the newspaper world prefer to be called copy editors while those in loftier realms opt for *copyeditors*. The fact that I, as a newspaper person, am bashing the non-newspaper usage is purely coincidental.)

As for the verb form, I favor *copy editing* (intransitive) and *copy-editing* (transitive): *She loves copy editing, but she wasn't eager to copy-edit this manuscript.*

DILEMMA I wish "Dr." Laura would tell her callers this: Not all problems are dilemmas. A dilemma is a choice between two equally attractive (usually unattractive) alternatives.

DISTRICT OF COLUMBIA Washington, D.C., is a city, not a state. Fourth-graders should know this, yet professional writers—even in Washington, D.C.—tend to ignore it.

WRONG: *Washington, D.C., ranked first among the states in a study of teenage pregnancy rates.*

RIGHT: *Washington, D.C., ranked higher than all 50 states in a study of teenage pregnancy rates.*

WRONG: *The District of Columbia was treated as a state for the study.* (It's best not to assume or imply that researchers have a sub-fourth-grade education.)

RIGHT: *The District of Columbia was ranked with the states for the study.*

The issue here goes beyond technical correctness, because it is inherently misleading to rank a city, especially an urban one, against the states. Even the most urban states, such as New Jersey, are largely rural and suburban, so the statistical effects of the big-city social problems of, say, Newark are diluted by square mile after square mile of farmland, suburbia and nothingness. Washington, D.C., has a good deal of parkland, but its population density remains much higher than New Jersey's.

DOMESTIC AND IMPORTED In the terms *domestic cars* and *domestic beer*, the word *domestic* means "made in the country we're now in." On American bar menus, however, the word is coming to mean "ordinary" or "inexpensive," as the quite domestic Samuel Adams and Pete's Wicked brands tend to be listed as "imported" alongside Heineken, Bass and Guinness rather than with lower-priced compatriots Budweiser, Miller and Coors. It will be a sad day, and cause for consumption of all of the above, when this mistake inevitably leaks into actual writing.

Dow On second or casual references, the Dow Jones Industrial Average is *the Dow*. The same "I want to abbreviate this, but I feel guilty about it" instinct that gives us *IBM Corp.* gives us *the Dow Jones*. Use the real name or use the common nickname, but don't be a weasel and shoot for something in between.

DOWNPLAY Purists will tell you that you must say "play down." That's fine, but you risk sounding stilted and antiquated. I say *downplay* is here to stay.

DRAFT BEER The verb *to draw* and the mispronunciation of *draught*, the British spelling of *draft*, have combined to lead some bartenders to pronounce the word like "draw," which has led some sign makers to advertise "draw beer." You can draw me a beer, thank you, but that doesn't make it a draw beer. It could be called a *drawn* beer, I suppose, but the word you're looking for is still *draft*.

DURING If you can substitute *in*, do so. You might think *during*, which features twice as many syllables as *in*, gives a sentence more power, but actually it tends to weaken things. Anyone can say something *during* the State of the Union address, but how many of us can say something *in* that speech? Sometimes, of course, that sense of detachment is precisely what you want: If a soldier served *during* the Vietnam War, don't change that to *in* unless that very different statement is true. (See WITHIN.)

EITHER You say "either"; I say "either." (Loses something in print, doesn't it?) My point here is not pronunciation, but parallel construction. Like *both*, *either* should be placed in such a way that it applies to both of the words it's supposed to apply to. It's easy to get this wrong when you're dealing with infinitive forms.

> **WRONG:** *It's important either to learn HTML or use a Web authoring application.* (The placement of *either* suggests that the *to* applies only to *learn*, and *use* is left hanging.)

> **RIGHT:** *It's important to either learn HTML or use a Web authoring application.* (The sentence is parallel because *learn* and *use* share a *to*.)

> **RIGHT BUT AWKWARD:** *It's important either to learn HTML or to use a Web authoring application.* (The *either* applies to both uses of *to*.)

E-MAIL It's not *email*, in case you haven't been paying attention to my vitriol on the subject. (Abbreviated explanation: Words based on single letters have never lost their hyphens, no matter how frequently they're used. It's *X-ray*, not *Xray*, *T-shirt*, not *Tshirt*, etc.) One update since "Lapsing Into a Comma": *E-mail* is acceptable as a noun meaning e-mail message (*an e-mail*, *several e-mails*). It's just too awkward to write *e-mail message* every time, and although you wouldn't write "The letter carrier brought me three mails today," there is no e-mail equivalent to *letters* or *parcels*.

ENGLISH PROFESSOR In speech, intonation makes it clear whether the phrase means *a professor of English* or *a professor who is English*. In writing, avoid the ambiguity.

-ER Judging from my e-mail, quite a few people get quite worked up if *[blank]er* is in the dictionary but someone dares to write *more [blank]*. Sure, you'll get deservedly pummeled on the playground if you say "My dad is more big than your dad," but am I really lazier and stupider than you if I occasionally choose to write *more lazy* and *more stupid*? The more complex an adjective or adverb gets, the more *more* becomes an option. Trust your ear: There's no reason that *grimmer* and *more grim* cannot coexist.

EXISTING HOMES Real-estate tip: Never buy a nonexistent home. Used cars are *used cars*, but used houses are what? The industry term is the silly-sounding *existing homes*, and you can get away with that, sparingly, in economic-indicators stories. A good way around the term, though, is *home resales* or *resale homes*.

A house is not a home, you say? Fair point, smarty-pants, but what about the sale of apartment-style condominiums? As I said in "Lapsing Into a Comma," I have no problem with *home* as an umbrella term for houses, apartments, condominiums, co-ops, mobile homes and whatever other forms housing may take.

EXPRESS WRITTEN CONSENT When the people at Major League Baseball warn against unauthorized "rebroadcast or retransmission" of their games, they're not erroneously leaving the *-ed* off *expressed*. *Express* is a perfectly good word meaning "explicit."

EXXON MOBIL The merged company is officially *Exxon Mobil Corp.*, but on its signs and its Web site it likes to refer to itself as *ExxonMobil*, without the space. Unless you want to confuse your readers with a very fine distinction, pick one. I say it's *Exxon Mobil* until the company decides to register a new name with the SecuritiesAndExchangeCommission.

THE FACT THAT The fact that many people consider this phrase inherently evil is unfortunate. It is unnecessary in many cases, but in other cases it provides emphasis and clarity. If I had begun the first sentence of this entry with *That*, as many writers and editors would, you would have been led down the wrong path, with *consider* appearing to be the verb until you got to the *is*, at which point you would have been forced to backtrack. "Oh! When he said *that*, he meant *the fact that*," you might have said to yourself. At least that's my theory.

FAST, SLOW When the road is clear, I like to drive fast.

If you're bristling at the idea of doing something *fast* instead of *quickly*, you're stuck in Adverb Amateur Hour. Now, stop humming the "Lolly, Lolly, Lolly" song from "Schoolhouse Rock" for a moment and pick up the dictionary: Dictionaries aren't always reliable guides to correct usage, but you can trust the entry that says *fast* and *slow* are adverbs as well as adjectives.

Quickly and *slowly* are also legitimate adverbs, but descriptions of driving speed veer into idiom territory because the speed of the driver's actions has nothing to do with the speed of the car. I can picture someone driving *quickly*—jamming the key into the ignition, releasing the parking brake and jerking the car into gear like Twitchy McTwitch on a Starbucks binge—but then proceeding down the road at 5 mph. The idioms that describe fast and slow driving are *driving fast* and *driving slow*.

FIRED   When Amalgamated Industries Corp., beset by quarterly losses, shareholder pressure and dwindling market share, decides to cut its workforce by 10 percent, do you think the supervisors bark "You're fired!" at the unfortunate casualties? Of course not, but that's the picture you paint if you write that these people were "fired." Although the word technically can apply to any dismissal, it carries the connotation of dismissal for cause. The alternatives have their own problems. *Downsized* is jargon. *Riffed*, from the acronym for "reduction in force," is even worse. *Laid off* is my choice. The term once applied primarily to temporary layoffs, but as the corporate world has made permanent layoffs its cost-cutting tool of choice, the idea of a temporary layoff has become rather quaint. If you mean temporary layoff, you can always say *temporary layoff*, as they do in the theme song from "Good Times."

THE FORESEEABLE FUTURE   How much of the future is foreseeable? A month? A week? (If it were any longer than a minute or so, wouldn't you be a stock-market billionaire?) This cliche is defensible only if you're writing for the *Miss Cleo Monthly*. It's *the near future* for the rest of us.

FOR EXAMPLE, FOR INSTANCE   I've known editors who differentiated between the two, but I don't see the point. There are better issues to waste your energy on.

FREE You get something *free*, not *for free*. The technical reason: It's an adverb, not a noun. If *free* alone looks naked to you in a particular sentence, there's always *at no charge*.

FRIENDS AND FAMILY You may not think you're parroting the commercials for MCI's discount long-distance rates when you use this phrase, but think about it: Are friends generally more important than family members? The logical way to write such a thing would be *his family and friends* or *her family and friends*. (Thanks to my brother Terence for pointing this out.)

GAME PLAY Video-game geeks use *gameplay* as one word. It means "game play," and I see no reason not to write it as two words in the real world.

GANDHI The last name of Mohandas K., Indira, Rajiv and other notable figures in India's history is misspelled with breathtaking frequency. It's not *Ghandi*.

GANG BANG, GANG-BANGER A *gang bang* is group sex, usually involving one woman and several men, while *gang-bangers* are roving bands of youth who violently fight each other. Avoid both terms until the perverts and the homicidal maniacs sort this thing out.

GENTLEMAN A writer isn't likely to write the way a diplomat speaks, but for the record, the generic term for a man is *man*. *Gentleman* went out a few decades ago, but you'll still hear it used, sometimes at inappropriate times, as in the 2003 news conference in which Secretary of State Colin Powell referred to the "gentleman" who was believed to have plotted the September 2001 terrorist attacks that killed about 3,000 people.

GIULIANI The former New York mayor is Rudolph Giuliani, not *Guiliani* ("gee-YOU-lee-ah-nee," not "GWEE-lee-ah-nee").

GRAND CENTRAL The New York train station is *Grand Central Terminal*. (*Grand Central Station* remains the correct expression for mothers yelling at their kids about running into and out of the kitchen.)

GROCERY STORE See SUPERMARKET.

HAD At the risk of being a "lint picker" (Theodore Bernstein's term), I must caution against references to people or entities *having* something done to them when that something was initiated by outside forces. *She had her car washed* is fine. *She had her car stolen* implies insurance fraud.

HAILS FROM Give me a break.

HAND I'm generally for conversational writing, but some habits of spoken English do not translate well to the written word. The superfluous *hand* in phrases like *upper left-hand corner* is one of them. People who need to refer to their hands to tell right from left don't tend to read much.

HARD-HIT, HIT HARD As with *rental-car companies* (see CAR-RENTAL COMPANIES), the familiarity of a derivative phrase is threatening to make the original phrase extinct. *A* *city hit hard by the hurricane* is, if you choose to turn that description into a modifier, *a hard-hit city*. No problem there, but that adjectival use has become so common that people are writing *A city hard hit by the hurricane*—not really an error, but certainly a twisting of the usual syntax.

HEALTHY, HEALTHFUL *Healthy* means "exhibiting health." *Healthful* means "giving health." So you can be healthy, but the diet that makes you that way is healthful. (If you're ready to pooh-pooh this often-ignored distinction, consider that a healthy appetite is often anything but healthful.)

HOMICIDE BOMBINGS Officials and advocates trying to shift the focus from suicide bombers to their victims coined this term, and they can have it. It's really more a play on words than a serious attempt at a better description. Doesn't *bomber* already imply homicidal intent? People who kill themselves and only themselves by taking pills or firing a gun are called *suicides*, not *suicide pill-takers* or *suicide gunmen*. And bombers of Timothy McVeigh's ilk are simply called *bombers*; the homicide is understood. Suicide bombings are called suicide bombings to set them apart from McVeigh-style bombings; if you think that somehow glorifies the bomber, I think you're nuts.

HOT-WATER HEATER I used to look at this term and think, "Well, *hot* water doesn't need to be heated, but that is what those things are called." But then I came to my senses. Repeat after me: "Water heater. Water heater." Sounds fine, doesn't it?

HVAC Do we really need another jargony abbreviation leaking into general usage? Let's leave this initialism for "heating, ventilation and air conditioning" to the heating, ventilation and air-conditioning people.

IBM Formally, it's *International Business Machines Corp*. The familiar form *IBM* is fine, perhaps even preferable, in casual references. (Plenty of people know what IBM is but don't know what it stands for.) But don't mix the two: There's no IBM Corp.

INBOX With the substantial increase in references to the place we look for our e-mail, the evolution from *in-box* to the solid form makes sense.

IN COLOR "The vehicle is blue in color," you might hear on a police scanner. As opposed to *smelling* blue? The phrase *in color* can usually be deleted from such descriptions, although you may want to keep it to avoid implying that something is made of, say, gold or silver.

IS IS *Is* can quite legitimately appear back to back as the end of an introductory clause and the beginning of a question:

> *The question is, is history going to look kindly on the Clinton presidency?*

The trouble is, people have gotten so used to hearing this that they impose it where it doesn't belong. People are starting to think the introductory clause is not *The [blank] is*, but *The [blank] is, is:*

> *My problem is, is, my husband likes to spend all his free time with strippers.*

So it was inevitable that we'd start to hear a *tripling* of *is*, and sure enough I have:

> *My question is, is: Is it normal for your 39-year-old cousin to show up at your front door naked?*

I need to stop listening to talk radio.

JAIL, PRISON This may not hold true in Mayberry-size towns, but convicted felons are generally sent to prisons. Jails are for misdemeanor offenders and people who have been arrested but not yet tried.

J.C. PENNEY J.C. Penney Co. brands its stores *JCPenney*. As with *Exxon Mobil* vs. *ExxonMobil*, I think it's silly to draw such a fine stylistic distinction between references to a company and references to its retail outlets. I use *J.C. Penney* for both.

K-9 UNIT Cops are so cute. But I believe the word is *dog*.

TO LAUNCH See TO SHIP.

LAYOFF See FIRED.

LEAD, LED A leader *leads* (present tense), a leader *led* (past tense), a leader *has led* (past participle). The past tense often erroneously appears as *lead*, probably because of an over-reliance on computer spell-checkers and the fact that the metal called lead is pronounced like *led*.

LEXIS, LEXUS How's this for modern, upscale potential confusion? *Lexis* is the spelling used by LexisNexis, the service that, among other things, archives newspaper and magazine articles. *Lexus* is the automaker, the luxury division of Toyota.

LIE DETECTOR If only such a thing existed! When people say "lie detector," they mean *polygraph*.

LISTSERV *Listserv* is a registered trademark for a brand of software to manage Internet mailing lists. Write *Internet mailing list* if that's what you're talking about.

LOCAL PHONE COMPANIES No hyphen. Local phone companies are phone companies that provide local service, not companies that provide local phones. To put it another way, it makes more sense to say *local* describes *phone companies* than to say *local phone* describes *companies*. By the way, AP style is correct in prescribing that *long-distance* keeps its hyphen when it's referring to phone service even if *phone service* is merely implied: *She uses AT&T for long-distance.*

LONG-STANDING, LONGTIME Dictionary trivia you should know: The first has a hyphen; the second does not.

MAGAZINE It can be reading material, or it can be part of a firearm. Not much chance for confusion there, right? Well . . .

When investigators got their big break in the 2002 D.C.-area sniper attacks, journalists reported that a suspect was identified through "fingerprints on a gun magazine." Ah, *gun* magazine, so it was the firearm definition. Nope. It was a gun magazine, as in a periodical about firearms that the suspect had leafed through at a convenience store.

What you write is always clear to you; good writers have the ability to read their words through an outsider's eyes and make sure it will be clear to others.

-MAN As most dictionaries recognize, a male jazz musician is a *jazzman*. A male oil executive is an *oilman*. The two-word forms represent much more casual relationships with jazz and oil: *"Do you prefer rock or jazz?" "I'm a jazz man." "Sunscreen or tanning oil?" "I'm an oil man."*

For a discussion of *-man* and gender-neutral language, see the "Madam Chairman and That Friggin' Masseuse" sidebar in Elephant No. 12.

MARKET We all know that radio ad salespeople are the coolest people in the world, but do we have to talk like them? *Market* is not an all-purpose synonym for *metropolitan area*. Use city plus *area*: *the Chicago area, the Omaha area, the San Diego area*. If you're selling something, fine, say "the Chicago market." But take my phone number off your damn list.

MERGERS When America Online Inc. bought Time Warner Inc., it became AOL Time Warner Inc. But don't let the existence of such a new name fool you into violating basic punctuation rules. Just as the fight between Lennox Lewis and Mike Tyson was the Lewis-Tyson fight, the merger of AOL and Time Warner was the AOL-Time Warner merger. The AOL-Time Warner deal (hyphen) produced AOL Time Warner (no hyphen), at least until the company decided to drop the AOL part.

MIAMI OF OHIO "Miami of Ohio" is a useful shortcut for sports reporters trying to avoid confusion with the Miami we usually hear about, but—like "The Times of London"—it's a misnomer. The Ohio school is simply Miami University. The Florida school is the University of Miami. (And the London newspaper is the Times.)

MOTORIST You'd think that I'd think that this is a stupid, made-up word for "driver." I thought that I'd think that, too. But then I read a newspaper article about a D.C. politician's altercation with a driver, and I immediately thought it meant "chauffeur." I have to conclude, then, that there are times when *motorist* is the clearer choice.

THE NEW YEAR *New Year's Day* is the New Year's holiday, but *the new year* is simply the new year. Lowercase. More important than the capitalization is the January tendency for journalists, like bill payers writing checks, to succumb to inertia and keep acting as if it's the old year. Business writers used to comparing quarterly earnings with those of the previous year, for example, need to switch off the autopilot and write "the previous year" instead of "last year" when it's the year 2525 and the quarter in question ended Dec. 31, 2524.

NOT UN- In his essay "Politics and the English Language," George Orwell scorns the *not un-* construction. He has a good point: If something is "not untrue," why not call it "true"? But not all descriptive words work in such a binary fashion. Sometimes something is not un-[blank] without being [blank]. Imagine Tom Jones singing "It's *usual* to be loved by anyone"—the line loses something in the editing, doesn't it?

OFF-BALANCE-SHEET ACTIVITIES The Enron affair taught us many lessons, and one of them involved hyphens. *Off-*

balance sheet activities describes what might happen in bed if you're drunk. Activities off the balance sheet are *off-balance-sheet activities*, with two hyphens.

ONLINE In "Lapsing Into a Comma," I called for *on line* and *on-line* but said I wasn't far from being swayed. Four years later, *online* looks right. (Who says I'm an old stick-in-the-mud?)

ONLY Careful writers are careful about the placement of this word, which can change the meaning of a sentence as it's moved away from what it's supposed to modify. *He only had three beers* is conversational and understandable, but technically it means *He had three beers and did nothing else.* In writing, *He had only three beers* is more precise.

Sometimes, though, you have to surrender to idiom:

I can only take so much of this!

OR The word is often misused in ranges:

He is expected to stay at the hospital for 10 or 20 more days.

Make that *10 to 20 more days.* (Obviously, the writer doesn't intend to rule out 11 to 19 days.)

In informal statements where two numbers are used hypothetically rather than as a true range, *or* is fine:

If I had 40 or 50 more workers, I could finish the project this week.

When the range spans only one unit, ask yourself whether the units are discrete or whether fractions of a unit may apply:

The pain can be relieved with one or two operations. (*Or,* not *to*—you couldn't have 1½ operations.)

The operation will take one to two hours. (*To,* not *or*—it could take 1½ hours.)

OTHER "No other pain reliever works faster!" a radio ad says. No need for *other* in that case; the analgesic in question can't work faster than itself, so the claim should be "No pain reliever works faster." But beware of the flip side of this error. If a statement is of the "There's nothing like it" variety, *other* is needed. No pain reliever works this fast? Uh-uh. No *other* pain reliever works this fast. There's nothing *else* like it.

PARTIAL QUOTES Use them if they're good and the full quote is awkward, but beware of writing that reads like a Zagat restaurant survey:

Greenspan said the economy "lacks vigor" and remains "in a sustained slump" but "may show signs of life next quarter" and "is still relatively healthy by historical standards." (Try the "superb" onion rings and the "melt in your mouth" cheesecake, but keep an eye on the "lazy" waitstaff and get a booth far from the "Siberia" back room.)

PARTICULAR In speech, this particular word is prized by people who love to hear themselves talk—it magically adds three precious syllables to any noun. In writing, *particular* often doesn't even have that much going for it. What does *this particular word* say that *this word* wouldn't have said? Nothing. *Particular* is sometimes useful, however, to avoid ambiguity. Compare *I was told not to say a word* with *I was told not to say a particular word.*

PARTNER There are worse made-up verbs, I suppose, but talking about one outfit *partnering with* another strikes me as gratuitous. *Team with* and other alternatives are readily available, and you can always sneak the words *partner* and *partnership* in elsewhere.

PEANUTS ON AIRPLANES It's a dated cliche, now that peanut allergies are all the rage. The up-to-date cliche would involve pretzels.

PER We love *per* and the superfluous *as per* in office memos (*Boom boxes are NOT allowed on desks during working hours, per Joanne*), but actual writing demands actual writing, and there are countless ways to actually write such a thing.

PERCENT AP's advice to always repeat *percent* in phrases such as *a 10 percent to 20 percent increase* strikes me as excessive. Repeat the word to avoid ambiguity: *The disease struck 10 to 20 percent of the Legionnaires* could conceivably be read to mean "between 10 Legionnaires and 20 percent of all the Legionnaires." But *a 10 to 20 percent increase* is clear, because "a 10 increase" is meaningless.

And don't get me started on the lunacy of imposing minor style conventions on quotes. If it strikes you as sensible to enforce such a guideline in a bracketed or parenthetical insert—*"Test scores ranged from 55 [percent] to 98 percent,"* *he said*—stand still for a moment while I strike you on the head with a bracket of the metal variety.

PERCENTAGES AND *OR* Percentages are useful for putting numbers in perspective, but the real numbers come first. Your stock fell $10 a share? Yikes! But if it's Berkshire Hathaway stock, that's not much of a drop at all. Still, the real number is the real number, and it should be treated with respect. Write *Berkshire Hathaway shares fell $10, or 0.01 percent*, not *Berkshire Hathaway shares fell 0.01 percent, or $10*.

PER SE It means "in itself." But beware: Even when used correctly, it marks a speaker or writer as a geeky, pretentious high-school student.

PLAN, PLANS Use the plural when the meaning is "intention": *The company's plans to buy the old warehouse were scuttled by the zoning board.* Use the singular when referring to an actual written-out strategy: *The company's plan for the new mall includes two department stores.* The preposition that follows the word is often a clue: Usually *to* goes with *plans* and *for* goes with *plan*.

PLAY DOWN See DOWNPLAY.

POP See SODA.

PORN Pornography is *porn*. Please don't say "porno," and please, please don't call a porn movie "a porno." I can't tell you exactly why *porno* is wrong, but I know it when I see it.

POWERPOINT Not *power point* or *powerpoint*. When people say "PowerPoint," they're not pointing out that someone's point was powerful. They're using the brand name of Microsoft's popular presentation software. Use the capital letters at the very least, and if it's not too clunky, use the manufacturer's name: *Microsoft PowerPoint*. (See also the "Everything's Generic" sidebar in Elephant No. 3.)

PRODUCT A product is something that's produced. Providers of services, ever envious of those who provide goods, are trying to get in on the fun. It doesn't work. Toaster? Product. Lamp? Product. Life-insurance policy? Mortgage? No.

If you've been to a hair salon in recent years, you know about the other *product* problem. "Would you like to try some product?" "Try a little more product to tame that cowlick!" As a mass noun referring to mousses, gels and pomades, *product* should stay in the salon.

QUARTER It can mean one-fourth, and it can mean the U.S. coin that is worth one-fourth of a dollar. Not much chance for confusion there, right? Well, there was the time I read a reference to a pharmaceutical company's *quarter-size patches* for delivery of medication through the skin. Were these patches one-fourth as big as a full-size patch? No, it was a reference to the coin. I made it *patches the size of a quarter*.

RHETORICAL QUESTIONS They're still questions (hence the name), so they get question marks: *Is this a great country or what?* Not so for observations that take the form of a question: *Boy, would I like a beer.* Polite requests and suggestions are trickier. Use a question mark if "no" could conceivably be the answer: *Would you mind scratching my back?* Otherwise: *Why don't you follow that advice and see how it works for you.*

ROUND TABLE, ROUNDTABLE A table that is round is a *round table.* The legendary round table of King Arthur is the *Round Table.* A group discussion is a *roundtable discussion,* or *roundtable* for short. Dictionaries differ on the discussion entry, but that's the way such nouns work. See BLUE BLOOD, BLUEBLOOD and YELLOW JACKET, YELLOWJACKET.

SAFE-DEPOSIT BOX Not *safety*. It's a box for the safe deposit of belongings. People say *safety* out of confusion because the first two syllables of the term—"safe-de"—sound like *safety*. The hyphen seems obvious to me (dictionaries agree), but I suppose the hyphen-phobic could dispense with it.

SAID, SAYS One of the great editing myths is that *said* and *says* can never appear in the same article. Each attributive verb has its place, and to insist on sticking with one or the other exclusively is a foolish consistency. *Says* tends to work better in a lede (first paragraph) or in a situation where someone is spouting a philosophy: *"I like boobies," Hefner says. Said* is the workhorse, to be used for quotations that apply to a specific situation, past or present: *"I have seven blond girlfriends," Hefner said. "Kimberly is my Playmate for life," he said at his 1989 wedding.* When in doubt, use *said*.

SAUDI ARABIA Watch out for *Saudia Arabia*, a common typographical error.

SAVE . . . OFF This is a problem of "ad-diction," as Bernstein called it, more than actual writing, but constructions such as *Save 50 percent off* are redundant at best. A sale can offer *50 percent off* or *50 percent savings*, but you save 50 percent *on* the merchandise.

SEEDING Many sportswriters seem to think *seeded* is the word that tennis people use to mean "ranked," the way tennis people say *love* when they mean "zero." Not quite. Seeding is the practice of arranging the draw for a competition so that the best competitors don't have to play one another until the later stages—the first seed can't meet the second seed until the final, the third and fourth seeds can't meet the first and second seeds until the semifinals, and so on. Seeding often coincides with ranking, but obviously it can't if one of the top-ranked players doesn't enter a tournament. Or maybe the Wimbledon people will make the No. 3 player the No. 9 seed because he's not very good on grass courts. So, please, Mr. Channel 2 Action News ex-jock, stop saying things like "Top-seeded Andre Agassi is skipping the tournament because of a wrist injury." Unless Agassi entered the tournament and then withdrew, he couldn't be seeded.

SERVICE, SERVICES As with *damage* and *damages*, you'll often see that extra *s* tag along where it isn't needed. If an airline reduces *services*, that might mean pretzels or beverages. Eliminating flights is a reduction in *service*.

SEVERANCE You say the company will offer severance when it lets people go? Of course it will! *Sever* in that context means *let go*. If you mean *severance pay*, say it.

SHE Girls and women are *she*. Ships and countries and hurricanes are *it*, unless you're going for the ever-popular old-coot-sea-captain effect.

SHIMMY, SHINNY You *shimmy* when you shake or vibrate. You *shinny* (or *shin*) your way up a rope or a pole.

TO SHIP "Your order has shipped," Amazon.com says. The next video-game sensation, DungeonSquat IV: The Quest for Ye Olde Golden Commode, "will ship next month," the manufacturer says.

Don't they mean the order "has *been* shipped" and the game "will *be* shipped"?

They do. They're doing the shipping; their products aren't. But the backward-intransitive trend, driven mostly by the high-tech world, is probably here to stay. *Launch* is often being used the same way: *The company launched in 1999.*

Defenders of these usages could cite instances that appear to be parallel. A book reads as if the writer is an arrogant jerk. (Ahem.) Something tastes good or looks good, although it's a person who's doing the tasting or looking. A car drives well, but it isn't doing the driving. But note the *as if* clause and the *good* and the *well*. Things don't simply read or taste or look or drive the way they are said to ship or to launch.

So the parallel is far from exact, and publications will have to make a close call on tradition vs. evolution. The less formal and more tech-oriented are likely to embrace *the product ships* and *the company launches*, while the more formal are likely to treat those usages with the same contempt that they would "Chunky is the soup that eats like a meal."

SHOCKED—SHOCKED! A day in the life of a writing fad:

Nonetheless, his audiences were shocked—shocked!—to learn that we Yankee rubes vote our judges into office. (Cleveland Scene, May 7, 2003)

Further rumblings of an ill-advised plan for a Shinnecock tribal gambling casino in Hampton Bays arrived this week at the same time as America was shocked—shocked!—to learn that virtue entrepreneur William Bennett has been a compulsive gambler. (Newsday, May 7, 2003)

Also on Sunday, Dick Van Dyke and Mary Tyler Moore starred in a new PBS production of "The Gin Game." D'ja see that? I was shocked—shocked!—to hear Rob and Laura Petrie using all that raw language. (New Orleans Times-Picayune, May 7, 2003)

Had enough? Me, too.

SHORT FOR, STANDS FOR Don't say an acronym or abbreviation "is short for" or "stands for" something unless you're certain that the relationship is straightforward. *BP* stands for *British Petroleum*; the company used the phrase "beyond petroleum" in an ad campaign playing off those initials, but in no way did *BP* ever stand for *beyond petroleum. R.E.M.* is the name of a rock band; it's also an abbreviation for *rapid eye movement*, a phase of sleep. The band's name was obviously taken from that abbreviation, but that doesn't mean the name stands for *Rapid Eye Movement.* An earlier (and inferior) rock band called Kiss styled its name in all caps, and some claimed, when devil worship was all the rage, that the name was not a reference to the act of affection but an abbreviation for *Knights in Satan's Service.* To say the name *stands for* that slogan is silly. Here's a tricky one: The Securities and Exchange Commission playfully christened a rule Regulation FD, with the *FD* part standing for *full disclosure.* But *Regulation FD* is not short for *Regulation Full Disclosure.* The regulation is simply called Regulation FD, in a nod to the way such rules are called Regulation A, Regulation B and so on.

SHORT-LIVED This is not a pronunciation guide, but I had to get this one in. *Short-lived* means having a short *life* (long *i*), not *living* (short *i*) a short time. It rhymes with *thrived.*

SODA People love regionalisms, so at the risk of spoiling your appetite for the meatier topics here, I'm going to discuss this one. Although as a Michigander I grew up saying "pop," I accept the fact that *soda* is the generic term for a carbonated soft drink in most parts of the United States. But please don't add the indefinite article. *A soda* means "an ice-cream soda" to me and many others. (Even if it didn't, it would be questionable. I would never say "a pop.") Use *a soft drink* or the name of the soft drink you're talking about (*a Coke*). And sorry, Southerners, but "a coke" as a generic term is indefensible.

SOLECISM Fancy-schmancy writers use this word for "usage error." I don't. You're welcome.

(I do, however, use *fancy-schmancy*. Sorry.)

SPECIAL What's so special about *special*? For one thing, it's one of the most overused adjectives in the English language. Stories about high-tech gadgets are especially *special*-y. A handheld organizer has a *special* attachment that turns it into a digital camera. A cellphone has a *special* attachment that allows it to connect to the Internet. Just tell me about the attachments and I'll decide how special they are.

SUPERMARKET The little place on the corner, the one run by the nice Korean couple, where I buy Budweiser, Ben & Jerry's and Glamour Kitty, is a grocery store. The Safeway a mile away is also a grocery store, but it's more accurately called a *supermarket*.

A TAD BIT *A tad* is fine. *A bit* is fine. For some reason, people like to redundantly pair the two.

THROUGHOUT THE COUNTRY Certain people have decided that *across the country* must be changed to *throughout the country*. I don't get it. *Across* isn't a perfect way of conveying the idea, but *throughout* seems more suited to a vat of liquid than to a land mass.

TIME-DAY-PLACE In informing readers about an event, the old rule is that the information should be provided in time-day-place order: *The meeting will start at 7 p.m. Thursday in the main auditorium.*

This strikes me as illogical, though, because the reader is first hit with a piece of information that is of little value. So what if it's at 7 p.m.? Will it be at 7 p.m. on a day when I'm still alive, or are you talking the year 2525? I have to keep listening to put that time in perspective. I prefer *Thursday at 7 p.m. in the main auditorium*, because then I get a logical narrowing-down progression. I can first focus on Thursday (am I even in town that day? am I working?) and then process the additional information to determine how that event might fit into my life.

TO See OR.

TOP-10 QUESTIONS Is it *top 10, top ten, Top 10, Top Ten, top-10, top-ten, Top-10* or *Top-Ten*?

It depends.

Top [x] can be a simple descriptive phrase (*Of all the usage errors I see, the top 10 are . . .*), or it can be a noun, sometimes a proper one, referring to an elite group of people, places or things (*The victory moved Notre Dame into the Associated Press Top 25*).

If you're not dealing with a proper noun, your style on numerals will decide the issue of *10* vs. *ten*. For this discussion I'll use Associated Press style, which spells out *one* through *nine* but uses numerals after that.

If the elite group is lowercased but is acting as a compound modifier, a hyphen is required: *Five top-10 players boycotted the tournament.* Skip the hyphen if you're treating the phrase as a proper noun: It's a *Top 10 player*, not a *Top-10 player*—unless the organization that invented the appellation chose to equip it with a hyphen.

Here's where things get complicated. You'd use a hyphen in *five top-10 players*, but usually not in *five of the top 10 players*. The top 10 players are top-10 players. A top-10 finish is a finish in the top 10. See what's happening? In its most natural form, *top 10* works like *10 best*: *The 10 best players are top-10 players*. It's only when *top 10* takes on a life of its own that it becomes a noun of sorts and therefore requires a hyphen as a modifier. Try that *10 best* substitution on the other side of that example—*the 10 best players are 10 best players*—and you'll see that it doesn't work. The lack of a conversational *the* is a clue that you're dealing with a label, a compound modifier, modifying *players*.

So, when *would* you use a hyphen in *five of the top 10 players*? When it's a second reference. If you had already mentioned top-10 players and then you meant five of *those* players, you would be correct to write *five of the top-10 players*. In general, though, the more conversational language you find around *top 10* (*the top 10 players in the world*, for instance), the less likely it is that the phrase should be hyphenated.

Some other examples:

Three of the top 10 players entered in the tournament lost in the first round.

Without a hyphen, it means that of the 10 highest-ranked players entered (their world rankings weren't necessarily in *the* top 10), three of them lost in the first round.

> *Three of the top-10 players entered in the tournament lost in the first round.*

With a hyphen, the sentence isn't answering the question "Three out of how many?" It's simply saying that of the players in the world top 10 who entered the tournament, three of them lost in the first round.

> *his top 10 victories*

Maybe he's beaten players ranked 21, 34, 39, 55, 81, 106, 111, 151, 160 and 188. Ten victories, but none of them against top-10 opponents.

> *his top-10 victories*

He beat No. 7 and No. 9. Top-10 victories, but nowhere near 10 of them.

One more thing: If *top 10* simply means "10 best," it takes a plural verb. If it refers to an elite group, it takes a singular verb.

> *The top 10 are playing this week.*

> *The top 10 is as strong as it's been in many years.*

TREASURYS U.S. Treasury securities are *Treasurys* for short, not *Treasuries*, under the general principle that proper nouns retain their spelling in the plural form (*the Grammys, the Emmys, the former two Germanys, what a bunch of Bettys*). There are well-established exceptions, of course, including *the Rockies.*

UNIQUE VISITORS Webheads writing for dimwits use this term to make it clear that multiple visits to a site by the same person are not counted as multiple visitors. Duh! Note my use of the terms *visitors* and *visits*. If you told me four of your relatives came over for dinner last night, I'd rule out the possibility that it was just one aunt and one uncle but both stepped out for a smoke at one point. *Visitors* means visitors.

WAIT'LL "Wait'll they get a load of me"? Uh-uh. In a contraction, *'ll* means "will." It cannot mean "till." *Wait till they get a load of me.*

WATER HEATER See HOT-WATER HEATER.

WEB, WEBBY, WEBCAM, WEBCAST, WEBCASTER, WEBHEAD, WEBMASTER, WEB PAGE, WEB SITE The World Wide Web is *the Web* for short. *Web* stays capitalized as long as it's its own word, but it loses the capitalization in legitimate compound forms and with suffixes, just as *Bible* becomes *biblical*, *Constitution* becomes *constitutional*, and *Congress* becomes *congressional*, *congressman* and *congresswoman*. Deciding when you're looking at a legitimate compound form is more art than science, but note the absurdity of *Web cast* or *Web head* or *Web master*. Although *cast*, *head* and *master* are nouns in their own right, those nouns are not in play here. It's the suffix: *-cast* as in *broadcast*, the (admittedly slang) suffix *-head* as in *stupidhead* and the suffix *-master* as in *ringmaster*. *Web site* and *Web page* remain two words just as *grave site* and *front page* remain two words; *site* and *page* act as full-fledged nouns, not suffixes. I use *webcam* as one word because the shortened form *cam* lends itself to compound forms (*minicam*, *digicam*), but that one is a close call. The adjectival *webby* is down like *congressional*, but don't confuse that with the uppercased *Webby Awards*.

WEBSTER The dictionary guy was Noah Webster, not Daniel.

And, by the way, there is no "Webster's Dictionary"; the Webster name is in the public domain, and many publishers use it. Merriam-Webster's Collegiate Dictionary is a descendant of Noah Webster's work. Webster's New World College Dictionary is also worth noting as the official dictionary of the Associated Press and most newspapers, but its *Webster's* is just a name.

WELCOME, WELCOMED *Welcome* in the sense of *a welcome respite* or *a welcome guest* is not an error. Things that are welcome are by definition welcomed as well, but to automatically tack on that *d* is an example of hypercorrection. (See EXPRESS WRITTEN CONSENT.)

WHIZ, WIZ The major dictionaries, uncharacteristically, avoid taking sides on which spelling is correct for the meaning "one who is especially skilled or gifted." So I guess I have to rule, and here's my ruling: Use *wiz*, short for *wizard*, except in the well-established term *whiz kid* (for which some dictionaries give *whizz kid* as an alternate spelling). So it's *chess wiz*, *computer wiz*, etc. And the pasteurized-process foodstuff that snobs disdain in every other context but require on a Philly cheesesteak is Cheez Whiz.

WILL The company will announce today . . .

Put away the crystal ball, and write only what you know: *The company plans to announce today . . .*

Morning newspapers on Sept. 11, 2001, were full of confident assertions that meetings "will" take place that Tuesday. Things change.

WITHIN As with *during*, if you can substitute *in*, do it. *Within the continental United States?* You're wasting a syllable: *In* means the same thing. *A decision is expected within four to six days?* No. If you mean *in four to six days*, say it. If you mean it could come at any time between now and six days from now, say *within six days*. (You've covered the bases: People know that four days is within six days.) *A deal could be announced within the next week?* No. *In the next week* makes perfect sense. *If the letter does not arrive within five business days, the deal is off?* Yes! That's what the word is for. The meaning isn't *in five business days*, because that would exclude one, two, three and four business days.

WHO The pronoun *who* refers to people. Avoid the common error of using it in place of *that* for companies or organizations. *That* should also be used in cases where a noun might refer either to inanimate entities or to people (*the manufacturers*, *the distributors*).

WHOSE *Whichse* isn't a word, so there's nothing wrong with using *whose* to refer to things in addition to people. You're free to nurse irrational pet peeves, of course, but please don't stoop to an awkward rewrite just to eliminate an inanimate *whose*.

 PERFECTLY ACCEPTABLE: *St. Louis, like New York and San Francisco, is one of those cities whose skylines are unforgettable.*

PROBABLY AN IMPROVEMENT: *St. Louis, like New York and San Francisco, has an unforgettable skyline.*

I DON'T THINK SO: *St. Louis, like New York and San Francisco, is a city of which the skyline is unforgettable.*

WORST NIGHTMARE What do you suppose would be a parent's worst nightmare? A child being tortured and killed? A child being tortured and *not* killed? Well, a major wire service says it would be the kidnapping *and eventual safe release* of a child. A major newspaper says it would be a toddler breaking an expensive computer! These are particularly ridiculous examples, but even a more nightmarish guess is still a guess. No writer can pretend to know what anyone's worst nightmare would be, so let's just avoid the stupid cliche.

WORTH Do you have *five years worth* of clutter in the garage or *five years' worth*? I vote for the apostrophe, because you'd use one with *a year's worth*. Things get trickier if you're using newspaper style for dollar amounts: The formal *ten million dollars' worth* is easy enough, but *$10 million worth* is best left alone—*$10 million's worth* is a big stretch to make a little style point.

YELLOW JACKET, YELLOWJACKET Dictionaries don't even mention *yellowjacket* as an alternate spelling, but in another call for civil disobedience, I say the insect, as opposed to the brightly colored windbreaker, must be one word. That's just the way nouns like that work. See BLUE BLOOD, BLUEBLOOD and ROUND TABLE, ROUNDTABLE.

YESTERDAY If news happens today and you're writing about it for tomorrow's newspaper, somewhere in the first paragraph you'll write *yesterday* or the day of the week or maybe even *today*, if your story begins with a dateline that contains today's date. Once you've done that, there's no need to specify that each person commenting on that very recent event is commenting very recently.

ZERO-PERCENT FINANCING *Zero-percent financing* sounds good in car ads, and "Why, it's *zero* percent!" might be an appropriate answer to the question "What percentage rate are you paying on your car loan?" Otherwise, there are better ways of expressing the idea. *No-interest financing* works, as does *interest-free financing*. Or you could simply call it *free financing*, just as you'd refer to something as "free" and not "costing zero dollars and zero cents."

A Web FAQ

There is no one-size-fits-all approach to references to Web sites. Philosophies differ, of course, but so do editing and typesetting systems, column widths, and interactions between print and online media—and all those things influence the local style decisions that publications must make. Here are 10 key questions on style and typography for Web references, plus some suggested answers.

Should Web sites' names be lowercased? No. Amazon.com, for instance, doesn't become amazon.com simply because typing the name into Microsoft Internet Explorer would cause a Web site to appear. The name *Amazon.com* is to the address http://www.amazon.com as *White House* is to 1600 Pennsylvania Ave. The convention with Web *addresses* (also known as URLs) is to use lowercase, but sites' *names* should be capitalized the same way as any other proper noun. Whether to reproduce a logo that uses all-lowercase or some other non-traditional capitalization is another topic, but suffice it to say that most well-edited publications reserve the right to capitalize the first letter of a proper noun (or at least the second, when *eBay* or a similar name appears midsentence).

One exception to the practice of lowercasing addresses: If a URL contains a slash other than the double slashes in *http://*, everything after that slash is case-sensitive. An address like www.stuff.com/MoreStuff.htm must be printed with that capitalization.

What if the name and the address are the same? Use the name. The Web bookstore is Amazon.com. It is not http://www.amazon.com   or   www.amazon.com   or   even amazon.com.

And if the name and the address are different? Use the name. Use the address, too, if you're directing readers to the site but not if it's just a casual reference. For in-between cases, you'll have to adopt a policy. Some publications prefer to publish Web addresses as a reader service; others prefer to avoid giving sites "free advertising." You may want to use both the name and the address—*Amazon.com (www.amazon. com)*—for the sake of consistency in an article that mentions other sites whose names and addresses are different.

Is there a good way to publish both a name and an address without it looking clunky? I like parentheses, as in *I run a Web site called The Slot (www.theslot.com)*. This way, you avoid the issue of whether it's misleading to tech-challenged readers to place a period immediately after a URL. It's pretty obvious what role the parens are playing. If you choose not to use parentheses and that issue does come up, by the way, the "sentences end with end-of-sentence punctuation" rule trumps any such concerns.

In a URL, are *http://* and *www.* necessary? Short answer: The *http://* is optional, but it's a good idea to keep the *www*.

Using the *http://* is a legitimate style choice, but to me it's anachronistic and a waste of space. One major exception might be if your publication feeds its copy to a Web site that depends on that *http://* to automatically generate a hyperlink when print copy becomes Web copy.

But if the only question is whether a reader typing in the characters as printed is going to get to the Web site in question, it's safe to assume that all domain-name servers and practically all browsers fill in the *http://* part automatically unless a different prefix is specified (*ftp://*, for file transfer protocol, and *https://*, for secure sites, must be included when you print addresses that use them).

Whether the *www.* is necessary to successful surfing, however, is unpredictable. DNS (domain name server) databases are often configured to route requests without the *www.* to the correct site, but those databases are always changing, and the DNS that your connection routes you to on Monday may not have the same database as the one you get routed to on Tuesday.

Why, then, do I advocate printing such site names as Amazon.com without that *www.* attached? Well, a site with *.com* in its name is more likely than other sites to have its DNS entries in order so that the name works as an address. When in doubt, you can always use the full address in parentheses next to the site name.

What if the address has no *www.*? Many publications choose to use the *http://* when there's no *www.*, under the theory that a Web address won't look like a Web address if it's printed with neither a *www.* nor an *http://*. That's a valid style decision, but I don't think the *http://* is necessary even in such a case:

> *For directions, try maps.yahoo.com.*

Should a Web address be italicized or boldfaced to set it apart from other text? That's another policy decision for your publication. Here's a look at the possibilities:

> The Treasury Department sells securities to the public through a Web site called TreasuryDirect (www.treasurydirect.gov).

Newspaper tradition points to this approach—treating the URL the same as other text. Where many publications would use italics, for instance, Associated Press style calls for either plain old type (as in newspaper and magazine names) or quotation marks (as in book and movie titles). AP's avoidance of italics has its roots in old technology—the inability of the newswires to transmit italics—but it has created a tradition that lives on even at papers that don't use AP style and are quite capable of producing italic type.

> The Treasury Department sells securities to the public through a Web site called TreasuryDirect (*www.treasurydirect.gov*).

> The Treasury Department sells securities to the public through a Web site called TreasuryDirect (**www.treasurydirect.gov**).

> The Treasury Department sells securities to the public through a Web site called TreasuryDirect (<u>www.treasurydirect.gov</u>).

If you choose to set off Web and possibly e-mail addresses, italics are the only realistic choice. Boldface sets things off a little too much and is traditionally restricted to specialized uses, such as columns about celebrities in which the celebrities' names might be highlighted. It would work for columns about the Web but not for regular general-interest copy. Underlining is an interesting idea, as it echoes the treatment of links on the Web, but the look would be jarring in print, and any publication that used it would be putting itself far outside the mainstream.

Remember, though: Even if you decide to use italics or some other special treatment for Web sites' addresses, the sites' *names* should remain regular roman type.

Is there anything else that can routinely be deleted from Web addresses? Yes. One is the trailing slash—*www.theslot.com/books/* can be printed as *www.theslot.com/books* without messing anything up. Also probably killable are the tags *index.html* and *index.htm*. Test an address to be sure, but generally those are default pages that appear automatically when the preceding www.whatever.com site is requested.

What's the best way to handle line breaks? This is another area where names and addresses of sites should be treated differently. When a line has to break, the *name* of a Web site should be treated as an ordinary word. Break on a syllable and with a hyphen:

> *In shopping for plane tickets, she tried Trav-elocity.com and Expedia.com.*

You'll sometimes see addresses treated the same way:

When her best friend told her about www.trav-
elocity.com/specials, she went to the site right away.

I think this is a bad idea. It might be underestimating the reader's intelligence to avoid hyphenating Web addresses, but there very well could be, say, a www.trav-elocity.com. When Travelocity.com is a name, the capital *T* and lowercase *e*, as well as the long-standing tradition of hyphenating actual words at line breaks, provide ample clues that the site is not named Trav-elocity.com. But the tradition that has evolved in the Web's short history is to avoid presenting addresses with possibly misleading hyphens, and the all-lowercase convention makes it more difficult to discern whether a hyphen is a line-break convenience or truly part of an address.

The ideal solution is to avoid line breaks entirely when dealing with URLs. In narrow newspaper columns, however, some breaks are inevitable.

A surprising number of publications dispense with not only the hyphen convention but also the syllable convention, breaking wherever a break would fit best:

When her best friend told her about www.traveloci
ty.com/specials, she went to the site right away.

Not to be judgmental or anything, but such a naked break is bad. Very bad. Even when syllables or even words are respected, naked breaks are not good:

When her best friend told her about www.travel
ocity.com/specials, she went to the site right away.

One valid style decision, and my personal choice, is to break after punctuation:

> When her best friend told her about www.
> travelocity.com/specials, she went to the site right away.

Breaking after a punctuation mark, especially if it's a slash or a hyphen, preserves the feel of a traditional hyphen break better than the other alternatives.

Some publications take a similar approach but break *before* punctuation:

> When her best friend told her about www
> .travelocity.com/specials, she went to the site right away.

That's also a valid style decision. There's that naked break, which I don't care for, but there's also the advantage of avoiding false-alarm periods (when the punctuation is a "dot") and ambiguous hyphens. A reader is probably less likely to think a Web address's real hyphen is nothing but a line-break convenience if that hyphen begins a line rather than ends one. It's a close call.

Is there some way to teach my computer system to follow that guideline on breaking Web addresses? Probably not. Ask your systems guru, but the best you can hope for is probably a "discretionary break point." You may be familiar with "discretionary" or "soft" hyphens—characters that you insert in a word to tell the system that if the word must be broken, here's where to break it. The CCI Word editing system at the Washington Post has the same sort of thing, only without the hyphen. Editors can insert this character after "dots" and slashes in Web addresses, and the system knows to break at those points if necessary.

BIBLIOGRAPHY

This is not intended to be an exhaustive list of the best usage guides and reference books, but here are the books that were piled next to my desk for consultation (or bookmarked as online references) as I wrote this book. In the case of the old-fashioned paper books, they are the editions I own; older or newer or harder or softer ones may be available.

The American Heritage Book of English Usage, Online Edition. Bartleby.com, 1996.

The American Heritage Dictionary of the English Language, Fourth Edition. Houghton Mifflin, 2000.

Associated Press Stylebook, Online Edition, edited by Norm Goldstein, 2003.

Bryson's Dictionary of Troublesome Words, Bill Bryson. Broadway Books, 2002.

The Careful Writer, Theodore M. Bernstein. Atheneum/ Macmillan, 1965.

The Chicago Manual of Style, 14th Edition. University of Chicago Press, 1993.

The Elements of Style, Third Edition, William Strunk Jr. and E.B. White. Macmillan, 1979.

Fowler's Modern English Usage, Second Edition, H.W. Fowler (revised by Ernest Gowers). Oxford University Press, 1965.

Garner's Modern American Usage, Bryan A. Garner. Oxford University Press, 2003.

Merriam-Webster's Collegiate Dictionary, Eleventh Edition. Merriam-Webster, 2003.

Miss Thistlebottom's Hobgoblins, Theodore M. Bernstein. Farrar, Straus and Giroux, 1971.

The New York Times Manual of Style and Usage, Allan M. Siegal and William G. Connolly. Times Books, 1999.

United Press International Stylebook, edited by Bobby Ray Miller, 1977.

The Wall Street Journal Guide to Business Style and Usage, Paul R. Martin. Wall Street Journal Books/Simon & Schuster, 2002.

The Washington Post Deskbook on Style, Internal Edition, Thomas W. Lippman et al., 2003.

Webster's New World College Dictionary, Fourth Edition. Macmillan, 1999.

Woe Is I, Patricia T. O'Conner. Riverhead Books/Berkley Publishing Group/Penguin Putnam, 1996.

Word Court, Barbara Wallraff. Harcourt, 2000.

Words Fail Me, Patricia T. O'Conner. Harcourt, 1999.

Words Into Type, Third Edition. Prentice Hall, 1974.

INDEX

About the Author

Bill Walsh, copy chief for national news at the Washington Post, lives in the Capitol Hill neighborhood of Washington, D.C., with his wife, Jacqueline Dupree. He was born in 1961 in Pottsville, Pa., and grew up in Madison Heights, Mich., and Mesa, Ariz. He received a bachelor's degree in journalism from the University of Arizona in 1984 and worked in a variety of reporting, editing and design positions at the Phoenix Gazette and the Washington Times before joining the Post in 1997. He served as copy chief in the Post's business section from 1998 to 2003. He has run the Web site The Slot: A Spot for Copy Editors (www.theslot.com) since 1995. This is his second book. His first, "Lapsing Into a Comma," was published in 2000.